MALCOLM HILLIER

CONTAINER GARDENING

THROUGH THE YEAR

MALCOLM HILLIER

CONTAINER GARDENING

THROUGH THE YEAR

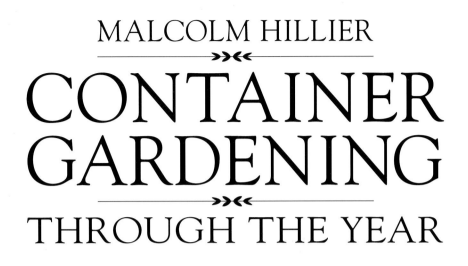

Photography by
MATTHEW WARD

DORLING KINDERSLEY
London • New York • Sydney • Moscow
www.dk.com

DK

A DORLING KINDERSLEY BOOK
www.dk.com

Project Editor Bella Pringle
Art Editor Louise Bruce
DTP Page Make-up Mark Bracey
Managing Editor Mary-Clare Jerram
Managing Art Editor Amanda Lunn
Production Manager Meryl Silbert

First published in Great Britian in 1995
by Dorling Kindersley Limited
9 Henrietta Street
London WC2E 8PS

First published as a Dorling Kindersley paperback 1998

Copyright © 1995, 1998 Dorling Kindersley, London
Text copyright ©1995, 1998 Malcolm Hillier

4 6 8 10 9 7 5

A CIP catalogue record for this book is available
from the British Library

ISBN 0-7513-0565-0
ISBN 0-7513-0172-8 Hardback

Reproduced by Colourscan, Singapore
Printed and bound in Singapore by
Star Standard Industries (Pte.) Ltd.

CONTENTS

FOREWORD 6

FOREWORD

GROWING PLANTS in hanging baskets, window boxes, troughs, pots, and tubs is immensely rewarding and offers great imaginative scope, particularly when gardening in the limited space of a patio, roof terrace, or balcony. Even in large mature gardens, container gardening offers seasonal colour and variety, and enables you to introduce plants to your garden that you would otherwise not be able to grow in the native soil.

— ❦ IDEAS FOR CONTAINERS ❦ —

A surprising number of plants, trees, and shrubs can be grown in pots, and grown well. I hope I can help you by explaining the principles of designing schemes for containers for a host of situations. I offer style guidelines for enhancing areas of the garden with imaginatively planted pots, be it a flight of steps, a doorway, a paved patio, a pergola, or a window-ledge.

   On the following pages, I have put together over 60 container creations for the garden, as well as ideas for inside the house and the conservatory. Focusing on each season in turn, I use a broad selection of plants that are readily available at nurseries and garden centres and are simple to grow.

FUCHSIA CANOPY

FRAGRANT IRIS

— ❦ PLANT PARTNERSHIPS ❦ —

For every featured project, I choose plants that are compatible in growing terms, look beautiful together, and complement the chosen container. While the main spearhead of the book is aimed at the summer months, when it is quite simple to achieve spectacular results, there are also plenty of plantings that will give of their best in spring and autumn. I also include planting ideas for indoors and outdoors to help you through the difficult winter months.

— ❧ *PRACTICAL ADVICE* ❧ —

Each planting scheme is supported by practical advice on how to grow the featured plants successfully. There is detailed information on the number of plants you will need to achieve a rewarding display of colour, the most appropriate potting mix, and the plants' water and food requirements. I also recommend the aspect in which they will thrive, whether sunny or shady, sheltered or exposed, and suggest a suitable garden location. I hope you get as much pleasure and inspiration from *Container Gardening Through the Year* as I have had putting together this selection of creative planting ideas.

BOWL OF PRATIA

INTRODUCTION

CONTAINER GARDENING has much to commend it but perhaps one of its greatest assets is its versatility. By growing plants in pots, you can provide temporary colour, where plants can be easily substituted once they are past their peak, as well as permanent interest through the year, with perennials, trees, and shrubs.

Raising plants and flowers in pots is especially useful for those with small town gardens or no garden at all. However, it is not simply an idea dreamt up to answer the gardening needs of people with limited space. Its value has been recognized for centuries in garden landscapes the world over, where stately containers filled with a myriad of plants were very popular.

— RAW MATERIALS —

Before detailing the planting schemes I have put together for spring, summer, autumn, and winter, I would like to introduce you to some of the raw materials available for container gardening, and to help you select the most suitable containers and plants for your needs. First, I will survey the decorative and functional merits of an array of containers, and then outline the advantages and disadvantages of the materials – clay, plastic, copper, or wood – from which they are manufactured. Lastly, I will guide you through the range of plants available to the year-round container gardener.

— BASIC GROUND RULES —

I would also like to share with you a few simple design guidelines that I try to bear in mind when planning my planting schemes: how to combine a number of pot and plant shapes to achieve pleasing proportions; how to use foliage and flower colours to create different moods; and how to mix different plant textures in displays for maximum interest and variety.

FRAGRANT MIX (*Left*)
In spring, a selection of clay flowerpots filled with hyacinths, grape hyacinths, and narcissus, looks especially welcoming on a sunny window-ledge.

SUMMER TROUGH (*Right*)
A shady corner of a balcony or patio can be brought to life with this vibrant summer planting of bright orange begonias, pale pink busy Lizzies, and old-fashioned pansies in shades of pale yellow and white.

CHOOSING THE RIGHT CONTAINER

Selecting the most appropriate container is every bit as important as choosing the plants to grow in them. Materials such as terracotta, fibreglass, stone, and wood all make wonderful containers, and most good garden centres carry a comprehensive range of designs. The classic pot shape has gently sloping sides that enable you to easily remove the plant and its root ball for repotting or planting out. Square pots are useful for plants with extensive root systems as they hold a greater volume of potting mix for their dimensions than conical pots. When selecting urns and jars, that are designed to taper towards the mouth, make sure that the container has a sufficiently wide planting area for your needs. For tall displays, opt for pots with heavy bases to prevent the planting from toppling over. And, if you prefer improvised containers, such as wheelbarrows, remember to provide a drainage hole in the base.

DISTRESSING TERRACOTTA

The appearance of most containers improves with age. To speed up the distressing process, paint some live cultured yoghurt onto the surface of the pot. Terracotta is very porous and soaks up the moisture quickly; stone pots will take a few days to dry out.

THE RESULT
Place yoghurt-painted containers outside in a shady position and, in a month or so, green moss will grow over the surface. Alternatively, place in the sun and the salts in the clay will leach out, forming a white patina.

RUSTIC WOODEN PLANTER

GLAZED CLAY POT

TERRACOTTA TOMS

TERRACOTTA BASKET

SELECTION OF CONTAINERS

*An array of pots in different shapes and sizes, made
from clay, stone, wood, fibreglass, and metal, gives
an idea of the choice of containers on offer.*

CONCRETE
CHIMNEY

TERRACOTTA
STACK

SWAGGED
TERRACOTTA POT

LEAD TUB

WOODEN TUB

FIBREGLASS
PLANTER

STONE
TROUGH

GLAZED
CLAY URN

COPPER POT

HANGING
BASKET

SQUARE
WIRE BASKET

TERRACOTTA
WINDOW BOX

TERRACOTTA POT (*Above*)
A time-worn terracotta pot hijacked by lichens and moss has a subtle beauty that does not overpower the delicate planting. Its faded surface blends comfortably with the beige and grey gravel path. With new clay pots, speed up the ageing process by following the technique for distressing terracotta outlined on p.10.

WOODEN VERSAILLES PLANTER (*Left*)
Tubs coated in wood preservative have a longer life. You can either buy then already treated, or paint them yourself with a clear wood varnish or coloured paint, depending on the desired effect.

— TRADITIONAL TERRACOTTA —

One of the most popular materials for pots has always been terracotta, which means that more pot designs are available in this than in any other medium. Plain or decorative, its rich, earthy colour combines beautifully with plants, and it weathers so well that its appearance often improves with age. Terracotta clay is a porous material and quickly soaks up water, so remember to water your plants in terracotta pots frequently, to prevent them from drying out.

If you live in a cold area, check that your terracotta containers are frost-resistant: pots imported from Mediterranean countries have a tendency to crack and flake. Unglazed and glazed stoneware is frost-proof and more water-retentive. Many terracotta pots are machine-made, but hand-crafted items are always more interesting. If hand-made pots are too expensive for your budget, carefully select mass-produced containers with slight irregularities as these often have greater character and appeal.

— NATURAL WOOD —

Wood is an attractive natural material for tubs, troughs, and window boxes, and a range of other containers. In damp regions, wood containers have a limited life unless they are made from hardwood. Softwood, however, can be treated with preservative to halt decay, or you can line wooden window boxes and tubs with plastic to limit rotting caused by watering.

Beer barrels and half barrels have always been popular plant holders. Now they are made especially for the gardener in a variety of shapes and sizes. Before purchase, check that the metal hoops around the barrel are fixed, and that there are no signs of warping.

RECONSTITUTED STONE PLANTER
A reconstituted stone planter soon darkens with age and its cast mouldings can easily be mistaken for expensive sculptured stone.

CONCRETE CHIMNEY POTS
Concrete chimney pots sprouting with ivy and weeds, and arranged on different levels, help to establish this unusual group of containers.

— LEAD AND COPPER —

Plants look particularly attractive in old lead and copper containers, especially when the surfaces of these metals develop a green-blue or grey patina on exposure to the weather. Although metal containers are expensive and very heavy, they last a lifetime. I buy antique containers in traditional designs at auction.

COPPER BOWL
To tarnish a bright copper surface, rub with wire wool and coat in vinegar.

— STONE AND FIBREGLASS —

Stone containers, like lead, are both beautiful and cumbersome. They look magnificent but need to be housed in a permanent site, as moving them about can be a strenuous task. Reconstituted stone or concrete are cheaper alternatives. They can look harsh when brand new, but treated with cultured yoghurt (see p. 10) they will soon resemble sculptured stone.

A number of fibreglass containers are designed to simulate natural materials; they are durable, inexpensive, and lightweight.

— IMPROVISED CONTAINERS —

Don't forget those objects that can be adapted to hold plants: chimney pots, wheelbarrows, and sinks can be modified to make containers that lend a special quirky charm to the garden.

CHOOSING THE RIGHT PLANTS

The secret of successful year-round container gardening is to plant a varied selection of trees, shrubs, and flowering perennials in pots to create a foundation of permanent plantings, and then to introduce annuals, biennials, and bulbs that can be easily changed once they are past their peak for temporary seasonal interest.

— SPRING BULBS AND SHRUBS —

Spring is an exceptionally rich season for the container gardener as a great number of bulbs grow fantastically well in window boxes, tubs, and troughs. To reap the rewards, plan ahead by planting up bulbs in autumn (*see p.148*). I favour bulbs that smell as good as they look, such as *Narcissus* 'Trevithian'. Early-flowering shrubs like camellias and rhododendrons will also thrive within the confines of containers, as will cherry trees and lilac, although these will not reach their full height. For extra spring colour, plant bulbs around trees and shrubs.

FRESH YELLOW AND PINK SPRING SHOW
Planted up in autumn, trailing evergreen foliage provides winter interest before the flowering of sweetly scented bulbs in spring. The planting will provide flower colour for three or four weeks.

— SUMMER ANNUALS —

By late spring, garden centres are teeming with annuals in a rainbow of colours. Many of them thrive in the controlled environment of containers, often performing better than in open ground if they are fed and watered at regular intervals. My summer container favourites include scarlet nasturtiums, pink pelargoniums, and orange begonias, as they provide a splendid show of colourful blooms over many weeks.

FLORIFEROUS SUMMER SELECTION
In summer, many annuals, such as busy Lizzies, petunias, and lobelias, flower simultaneously. With judicious planning and grouping of containers on different levels, you can easily achieve a spectacular show of colour and fragrance that spans several months.

— AUTUMN FLOWERS AND BERRIES —

Many of the summer annuals produce a further crop of flowers in autumn. Fuchsias, busy Lizzies, and begonias all put on particularly strong shows of autumn flowers. A few plants, such as Michaelmas daisies, chrysanthemums, and autumn-flowering gentians, come into their own at this time of the year. It is also a good season for berries: pyracanthas and cotoneasters grow well in containers.

AUTUMN DAISIES
(Right)
Osteospermum flowers have a second lease of life in autumn. Mixed with rust-leaved coleus they produce a gloriously autumnal effect.

— WINTER EVERGREENS —

Throughout the year evergreens are invaluable, providing a leafy foil to the more seasonal plants. In the harsh winter months evergreens, such as box and privet, are useful. Clipped into simple geometric shapes they add an architectural beauty to paved patios and pathways. In warm winter spells, I often stand pots of cyclamen and azaleas on a table outside my kitchen window, but remember to bring them indoors as soon as the temperature drops. During winter, make container plantings a feature in your home. Hyacinths and narcissus can be encouraged to flower early and, if you are lucky enough to have a garden room or airy conservatory, you could grow winter-flowering jasmine for its fragrance.

WINTER WINDOW BOX
Situated on a sheltered window-ledge, winter-flowering heathers and pansies will put on a brave show during milder winter spells.

AROMATIC KITCHEN HERB GARDEN
*Most herbs have Mediterranean origins and favour a bright site.
Here, variegated lemon balm sits amidst a bed of culinary herbs.*

SUN-LOVING NASTURTIUMS AND MARIGOLDS
*A wooden trough brimming with scarlet nasturtiums, marigolds, and
purple cabbage leaves flourishes in a bright sunny location. Water
the planting regularly to prevent the potting mix from drying out.*

— CHOOSING THE RIGHT SITE —

When choosing plants for containers, the aspect
of the intended site, be it bright, shady, sheltered,
or exposed, should be at the forefront of your
mind. Plants in pots are naturally more exposed to
the elements than plants growing in flowerbeds, so
the more adept you are at matching the plants'
needs to the limitations of the site, the more
successful your plantings will be in the long term.

— BRIGHT SITES: SUN AND SEMI-SHADE —

The majority of plants and flowers growing in
open ground perform best in bright sites that
receive direct sunlight for all or most of the
day. When planted up in pots, however, even
those varieties that are known sun-worshippers,
such as pelargoniums, grow better in sites
where they have respite from the sun. This is
because container-grown plants, especially
those in hanging baskets, have less soil to retain
water; only regular watering will prevent leaves
and flowers scorching in very hot sunny spells.

Areas of a courtyard and north-facing window-sills are often in shade for some, if not all, of the day. Surprisingly, many colourful plants – begonias, hydrangeas, busy Lizzies, azaleas, and rhododendrons – grow well in semi-shade.

— SHADY POSITIONS —

The most problematic sites are those in deep shade, cast by a tall building or leafy tree. Consider painting garden walls white to reflect light, and plant pots of bright white-coloured bulbs, such as hyacinths, that are shade-tolerant.

— SHELTERED AND EXPOSED SITES —

Protected sites are usually found beside walls or other features that act as a wind-break and provide shelter from strong sun and rain. In built-up areas, the temperature is often a few degrees warmer than in outlying areas, and so it is possible to grow a range of tender plants. Exposed sites are much more difficult. If there is nothing you can do to create shelter, try planting tough Mediterranean plants in well-drained soil, or select low-growing perennials that will not be battered by wind. Succulents are also resilient to exposed conditions.

EXPOSED ALPINE TROUGH (*Right*)
In early spring, saxifrages, phlox, and stonecrops – all native to snowy alpine landscapes – grow well in exposed sites.

LOW CAULDRON (*Below*)
Hardy plants, such as scabious and erigeron, grow well in the same container for two or three years. They require little maintenance, and their low-growing habit makes them wind-resistant.

FLOWERING AZALEA FOR SHADE (*Above*)
An azalea, planted in a large tub, produces a profusion of ice-pink flowers, bringing instant colour to a shady spot. It will flower for several weeks, and then again in successive years.

PLANTING FOR COLOUR

Colour is very much a matter of personal taste, but when planning schemes for containers an awareness of the mood colour combinations create is important. The colour wheel, through which the key principles of colour theory are explained, can be used for understanding the effects of colour in the garden: red, orange, and yellow evoke a feeling of 'warmth', while purple, blue, and green create a 'cool' effect.

THE COLOUR WHEEL (Right)
Warm colours are those the mind associates with the sun and a sense of well-being; cool colours evoke a soothing, tranquil mood.

WARM COLOURS

COOL COLOURS

HOT RED AND YELLOW COLOUR COMBINATION
An effusive mix of pillar-box red, cerise pink, and sunny yellow create a vibrant mix that sings out against brilliant green foliage.

COOL BLUE AND GREEN COLOUR MIX
A harmony of purple-blue hydrangea flowers and green foliage enhances the cool mood of this shady corner of a courtyard.

HARMONY

Harmonious mixes are achieved by combining dark, medium, and light tones of one pigment, or by mixing plants whose colours sit next to one another on the colour wheel.

TONES OF RED (*Above*)
Establish harmony by combining a range of dark and light tones of one colour. In flower terms, a mix of reds and pinks has this effect.

SUNSET HARMONIES (*Above*)
Flowers and berries in reds, oranges, and yellows – colours that sit next to one another on the colour wheel – are truly harmonious.

PINK AND PURPLE HARMONY
Closely harmonious pinky purple and lilac-blue combine to produce a soft misty effect that works well with the glazed plum-red container.

CONTRAST

Complementary colours are created by mixing hues that sit diametrically opposite one another on the wheel, such as red and green. Colour contrasts are those that do not share a common pigment, such as blue and yellow.

COMPLEMENTARY COLOURS (*Above*)
Bright red flowers and green foliage can be optically exhausting. Add gold, purple, or red-tinted foliage to tone down the colours.

PURE CONTRASTS (*Above*)
When working with contrasting colours, use paler colour values rather than pure hues, and soften the contrast with green foliage.

CONTRAST TO ORANGE
Vivid orange and deep violet hues create a lively contrast when used in container plantings as these two colours share no pigment in common on the colour wheel.

PLANTING FOR PROPORTION AND SHAPE

Plants grow in a variety of different shapes and sizes. To select the most suitable container, and then location, you need to consider a plant's natural habit – upright or trailing, for example – and how tall the plant is going to grow, either in a single season, or until it needs repotting.

When buying shrubs and perennials, always check the dimensions of the plant written on the label; annuals are not labelled for size so you may have to consult a reference book.

GRAND-SCALE TROUGH
The solid rectangular shape of an antique lead trough is filled with a mound of flowers and foliage that perfectly balance its proportions.

The shape of the pot and planting should look comfortable together. As a visual guideline, plants in containers should not be more than twice the height of the pot, or more than half as wide again as the width.

When grouping a mixed selection of container plantings, their shape, size, and number should be proportionate to the site. Ensure that they form close-knit groups, and that they sit at a number of different levels for added interest; one large container can often create a more pleasing shape than a group of small pots scattered disparately over an area.

— SIX BASIC PLANTING SHAPES —

To achieve pleasing proportions in container displays, it is helpful to bear in mind the six basic design shapes outlined below.

Fan-shaped displays work well in conical pots as the plants grow up and spread out into a bushy fountain of flowers. The second basic shape is a simple rectangle. It can be either vertical, when growing upright plants in a wide pot, or horizontal, if you are using a window box or long trough. Both oval- and dome-shaped plantings work well in low-level containers where they can be viewed from above. They should look just as good from the back and the sides as they do from the front. Although rather difficult to achieve, as you can never quite predict the speed or direction of natural plant growth, try altering the centre of balance in a display by creating a simple asymmetrical design in a symmetrical container.

1. FAN-SHAPED
Plants and shrubs that splay out into an attractive fan shape work well in terracotta pots that are conical in shape. Select plants that grow to about one and a half times the container height for a balanced display.

2. VERTICAL
To create visual symmetry, try to grow several tall plants together in a single container so that the width of the plants equals the width of the pot. Plant seasonal annuals or foliage around the base.

3. HORIZONTAL
To counteract the long, narrow shape of a window box or trough, avoid planting in straight rows, vary the height of the main plants to break up the horizontal thrust, and soften the overall effect with filler plants.

4. OVAL-SHAPED
Oval-shaped containers are often low-level and so look most effective when viewed from above. Plants that are diminutive in stature, or have a characteristic spreading or trailing habit, are the most suitable candidates.

5. DOME-SHAPED
Many plants grow into hummocky shapes, a profile that suits low tubs and cauldrons in exposed sites. Here, trailing foliage helps to break harsh outlines, while allowing some of the container's decorative surface to be seen.

6. ASYMMETRICAL
Although perhaps one of the more difficult shapes to achieve, as the proportions of plant material are not equal, asymmetrically planted displays have a movement and vitality lacking in more traditional designs.

PLANTING FOR TEXTURE

The ability to work with different flower and leaf textures is as much the key to successful container plantings as an awareness of colour and shape. Your choice of textures is governed by where you intend to place your pots. Small feathery leaves and dainty little flowers create delicate plantings whose subtle beauty can be appreciated close to, but, to create a display that can be appreciated from a distance, work with bold flowers and large leaf shapes. When working with groups of containers, I often choose pots in similar styles to focus attention on the different foliage and flower textures.

BOLD FLOWERS AND DELICATE FOLIAGE (*Above*)
Large red vallota flowers set against a background of dainty silver helichrysum and rosettes of succulents dominate this group.

ESTABLISHING TEXTURAL BALANCE (*Below*)
An equal mix of bold waxy flower and leaf shapes, and smaller feathery flowers and foliage, creates a perfectly balanced selection.

Once you start to look closely at the plants, it becomes clear that flower petals and leaves come in a staggering range of textures. They encompass everything from waxy, smooth, and shiny to matt and prickly, with all the subtle variations in between. When planning displays, try and bear this in mind, and arrange groups of containers at different heights to show off the variety of textures to full advantage.

MIXING FLOWER TEXTURES AND SHAPES (Above)
Here small and large flowerheads in shades of pink create a delicate small-scale planting. Clusters of polygonum pom-poms and papery thin pelargoniums and phlox mix with velvety petals of cerise petunias.

COMBINING A VARIETY OF LEAF TEXTURES (Left)
A variety of leafy textures, shapes, and colours creates an interesting display for a shady site. Waxy dark green begonia leaves combine with variegated curlicues of houttuynia, and trails of lysimachia.

GROUPING FLOWERS AND FOLIAGE (Right)
A spring group of cylindrical pots demands attention with a series of textures that are strongly at variance with each other. The mossy saxifrages, with their frail-stemmed flowers, stand before an ice-pink rhododendron with strong branch shapes and waxy dark green leaves. The frilled green ruff of primula leaves relates well to the strap-shaped foliage and fluted waxy flowers of arum lilies.

SUITING ARRANGEMENTS TO LOCATIONS

The objective of all container gardeners is to match a single pot or group of containers with the given surroundings. A theme that I cannot stress strongly enough is that the success of your plantings will rest upon your ability to interpret the potential and the limitations of the site from the beginning.

With this in mind, you can choose plants that thrive in the given aspect, select pots made in materials that blend harmoniously with the surroundings, and tailor the shape and scale of your planting so that it sits comfortably within the dimensions of the site. As with most things, common sense and forward planning play a large part. It is all too easy to plant up some

CLASSICAL FORMALITY (*Below*)
A grand moss-covered urn on a pedestal, filled with vivid pink pelargoniums, creates an air of formality in this extensive garden.

pots of plants to stand along a path, only to find that within a season they have grown too wide, obstructing the passage of passers-by.

— ACCESSIBLE SOLUTIONS —

Practical considerations should influence your decisions when planning arrangements for narrow doorways, small windows, and shallow flights of steps. With high-level plantings in particular, make sure that you choose wide window-ledges and balconies and that you have secure moorings. Check that plantings can be reached for watering and general maintenance.

— QUICK REMEDIES —

Container plantings can be used as quick expendable remedies for a number of location problems. For example, containers filled with colourful flowering plants can be dropped in to fill a bare, unsightly hole in a flower border, and tall trees or bushy shrubs planted in pots can create an instant windbreak and protect vulnerable plants growing in flowerbeds.

— INTERPRET THE MOOD —

A specific location may suggest a mood or a theme that can be enhanced by your choice of container plantings. For example, in a garden room you may wish to establish an eastern flavour by planting exotic orchids in clay urns. In a sunny brick courtyard you may be inspired to create a relaxed Mediterranean feel by cramming terracotta pots of pelargoniums into every available space, while loggias and poolside sites take on a classical air when surrounded by pots of clipped box and yew.

SPANISH STEPS (*Right*)
Decorative pots of pelargoniums form an avenue of colour up a flight of stone steps. The relaxed welcome they create contrasts with the formal use of the same flowers in the stone urn (Left).

SPRING

*W*ithout doubt, spring has to be the most exciting time of the gardening year as we anticipate the warmer weather to come. Gradually, dreary cold winter days dissolve into lighter mornings and evenings, and crocuses, daffodils, and cherry blossom sit against a background of pale blue skies. Soft pastel shades are the predominant hues in nature and these are echoed in spring plantings. Choose pale creamy yellow primroses and narcissi, and blue-flowering bulbs such as hyacinths and scillas. Their soft shades and perfumes are as fresh as the spring breezes, and nothing later in the year quite matches up to them.

❧❦

PASTEL HUES
Ice-blue pots are planted up with the pastel flowers of pale pink cherry blossom, pale blue grape hyacinths, and yellow primroses, narcissi, and trailing variegated ivy. (See p.46 for details.)

CAMELLIA, AZALEA, AND HYACINTHS

☀ SEMI-SHADE 🛢 MEDIUM-RICH AND ACID POTTING MIXES ⚱ MOIST CONDITIONS

JUST AS THE SCENT of the hyacinths begins to perfume the air, the evergreen azalea and camellia shrubs start to put on their spring show. What better way to celebrate these firm favourites than to grow them as a group: I have created a riot of colour by combining bright delphinium-blue and cardinal-red hyacinths, a deep crimson azalea, and a shell-pink camellia against a backdrop of dark green leaves. Place the group of terracotta pots on a patio or terrace; they will thrive in the same containers, without replanting, for several years in succession.

HYACINTH
*Hyacinthus 'Blue Skies'
is, in my view, one of the best
blue hyacinths available;*
● 12 bulbs.

AZALEA
*Rhododendron
'Vuyk's Scarlet'
grows very well in pots,
and bears brilliant red
flowers in late spring;*
one shrub. ●

HYACINTH ●
*Hyacinthus
'Hollyhock' has
double, brilliant
scarlet flowers. After
flowering, plant out
in the garden for the
following year;*
12 bulbs.

*Terracotta pot; ●
40cm (16in) deep,
40cm (16in) wide.*

Height
1.1m
(3½ft)

*Terracotta pot ●
33cm (13in) deep,
33cm (13in) wide.*

◆ GROWING TIPS ◆

Both azaleas and camellias can be
planted throughout the year, and
require acid soil. Neither shrub
tolerates low temperatures, and in
cold conditions both are best kept
indoors. Plant up the large pot of
hyacinth bulbs during autumn, in
a medium-rich potting mix.

CAMELLIA
*Camellia japonica 'C.M. Wilson'
has beautiful double shell-pink
flowers. Always keep just moist;*
● one shrub.

IVY-LEAVED TOADFLAX
*Cymbalaria muralis 'Globosa
Rosea' produces small lilac flowers
in late spring and summer;*
seven plants. ●

TRAILING IVY
*Hedera helix
'Heron's Foot'
has narrow glossy
dark green leaves;*
● four plants.

*Toadflax's trailing habit ●
makes it well suited to growing in
pots; plant up in early spring.*

*Moss-covered terracotta
pot; 80cm (32in) deep,
● 42cm (17in) wide.*

BOWL OF PRIMULAS

☀ SUN/SEMI-SHADE ⬛ MEDIUM-RICH POTTING MIX ⬚ MOIST CONDITIONS

T HE PRIMROSE, THE COWSLIP, the polyanthus: many different types of primula are available at garden centres and many of them flower in spring. The varieties in this bowl planting make ideal companions as they enjoy the same growing conditions and have the same flowering period. Polyanthus, whose cerise flowers form the bulk of this display, are available in a brilliant range of vibrant colours. And as a bonus, they also have a sweet scent.

◆ GROWING TIPS ◆

Plant up this selection of primulas in autumn. Place the bowl in a sunny or semi-shaded position and deadhead regularly to encourage new flowers. Water occasionally to keep the soil just moist. After flowering, transplant all the plants into the garden to free the pot, but beware of slugs and snails, as they love primulas.

POLYANTHUS
Primula Pacific Series bears sturdy sweet-scented flowers. Buy plants of this garden hybrid as a mix or as separate colours; six plants. •

COWSLIP
Primula veris has lightly perfumed yellow flowers borne on tall stems;
• six plants.

• POLYANTHUS PRIMROSE
Primula vulgaris 'Eugénie' is a double purple-blue primrose; three plants.

Small terracotta bowl; •
15cm (6in) deep,
45cm (18in) wide.

Height
60cm
(24in)

FRITILLARIES AND FERNS

☼ SUN/SEMI-SHADE ⚒ MEDIUM-RICH POTTING MIX ⚏ MOIST CONDITIONS

BOTH FERNS AND FRITILLARIES are great favourites of mine. They thrive in the same conditions so I love to team them up. It is wonderful to see the buds on the tall stems of the snake's-head fritillaries open to reveal nodding bells of exquisite petals with the most beautiful snakeskin markings. The graceful ferns unfurl at just about the same time, to reveal brilliant fronds of spring green foliage.

◆ GROWING TIPS ◆

Plant both fritillary bulbs and ferns in autumn. Grow in a well-drained potting mix, and keep moist though not soggy, especially in cold winter weather. This planting can remain in the pot throughout the year, or you can plant out several fritillary bulbs among wild grass in the garden.

SNAKE'S-HEAD
FRITILLARY
Fritillaria meleagris,
a white-flowered form;
eight bulbs. •

SNAKE'S-HEAD FRITILLARY
Fritillaria meleagris has
chequered markings with a
pink, lilac, purple, or white
• *background;* 17 bulbs.

• *Snake's-head*
fritillary can be
found growing
wild in river
meadows and
pastures.

FERN •
Polypodium
vulgare
'Cornubiense'
is an evergreen fern
grown for its
sculptural form;
three plants.

• *Fluted terracotta bowl;*
20cm (8in) deep, 35cm (14in) wide.

Height
50cm
(20in)

BASKET OF KALANCHOE

☼ SUN/SEMI-SHADE 🌡 MEDIUM-RICH POTTING MIX 🍴 DRY CONDITIONS

FOR THE HOUSE OR CONSERVATORY, the succulent *Kalanchoë pumila* is a magnificent-looking plant that combines beautiful silvery pink foliage with a profusion of pale pink spring flowers. Another perhaps better known kalanchoë, available at garden centres, is *Kalanchoë blossfeldiana* or flaming Katy. Considerably taller than *K. pumila*, it has many hybrids in a range of colours. I grow *K. pumila* on a bright window-sill during winter then, once the chance of frosts has passed, place the display in the garden in semi-shade; it comes indoors again in autumn. Kalanchoë is ideally suited to growing in a basket as it has a low spreading habit.

◆ GROWING TIPS ◆

Plant up this frost-tender succulent in late summer so that it will be well established by the following spring. Grow in a well-drained potting mix in a site with plenty of bright light, but not direct sun. In winter, keep the plants quite dry and moderately warm. During the spring and summer growing season, water lightly and feed every week. For best results, repot kalanchoë annually in spring.

KALANCHOE
Kalanchoë pumila has tubular pink flowers, 1cm (½ in) long, that appear in early spring; three plants. ●

Serrated-edged leaves are coated ● *in a white film.*

SILVER MOSS ●
conceals the plastic container in which the kalanchoë is planted.

● *Wire basket, 28cm (11in) deep, 28cm (11in) wide.*

Height
38cm
(15in)

Sweet-perfumed Iris

☼ SUN/SEMI-SHADE 🌱 MEDIUM-RICH POTTING MIX ✧ MOIST CONDITIONS

THE IRIS ARE AMONG my favourite flowers. Bearing the name of the Greek goddess of rainbows, their beautifully formed blooms shimmer in myriad colours from clear yellows through true blues, lilacs, and purples, to deep reds and browns. Many are scented with a perfume reminiscent of Parma violets. These reticulata irises are particularly beautiful, and are easily grown from small bulbs. They are short in stature, and most forms flower in early spring. A sunny garden table is the perfect site to display their blue, purple, and white flowers.

◆ **GROWING TIPS** ◆
Plant up the iris bulbs in autumn, and position in a bright but sheltered site. Water regularly to prevent the bulbs drying out but not during cold spells. After flowering, feed the planting at three-monthly intervals to ensure good bulbs the following year.

• *After flowering, the leaves grow to twice their present height.*

RETICULATA IRIS •
Iris reticulata is a hardy miniature variety of iris;
50 bulbs.

Low terracotta saucer;
10cm (4in) deep,
30cm (12in) wide. •

Height
25cm
(10in)

PANSY AND DAISY HANGING BASKET

✲ SUN/SEMI-SHADE   🌱 MEDIUM-RICH POTTING MIX   🍴 MOIST CONDITIONS

FOR THIS DELIGHTFUL hanging basket, I've chosen pink, violet, and purple pansies mixed with white daisies. Spring pansies are particularly good for this outdoor display of colour as they prefer the cool weather at this time of year and, unlike many other spring-flowering plants, they have a sprawling growth that will fill the basket. Double daisies make ideal companions for the pansies as they are at their best in spring.

◆ GROWING TIPS ◆

Plant up the basket in late autumn and, with luck, you will have a few pansies flowering during mild winter spells. Alternatively, plant in early spring and the display will flower for a month or more. In early summer, the spring pansies and daisies finish flowering but you can use the ivies again in another planting.

Hanging basket lined with moss; 15cm (6in) deep, 40cm (16in) wide.

DOUBLE DAISY
Bellis perennis 'White Carpet', a large-flowered cultivar, is easily grown to produce a mass of blooms; four plants.

PERSIAN BUTTERCUP
Ranunculus asiaticus grows from a tuber and tolerates light frost; two plants.

TRAILING IVY
Hedera helix 'Harald' is a compact variety; three plants.

PANSY
Viola x wittrockiana Universal Series is available in many colours, and flowers in winter and spring; eight plants.

Height
60cm
(24in)

WOODLAND WINDOW BOX

☼ SUN/SEMI-SHADE   ⚱ MEDIUM-RICH POTTING MIX   ⚖ MOIST CONDITIONS

I LIKE TO GROW spring plantings with a foundation of evergreen foliage to give winter interest before the arrival of the flowers. Here, the periwinkles and ivies have variegated leaves and the primulas display attractive leaf rosettes. During late winter, the narcissi start to push through the soil and, by mid-spring, the window box is brimming with sky-blue, pink, and pale yellow flowers. What's more, the display will give you pleasure for as long as three to four weeks.

◆ GROWING TIPS ◆

Plant up this window box in autumn. If you grow greater periwinkle in your garden, lift small clumps and transplant them into the window box. Plant the small narcissus bulbs 5cm (2in) deep and close together in small groups, between the primulas and periwinkles. Deadhead flowers regularly and tidy up fading foliage.

NARCISSUS
Narcissus triandrus 'April Tears', 25 bulbs.

● DRUMSTICK PRIMULA
Primula denticulata has globes of pink flowers; three plants.

GREATER PERIWINKLE
Vinca major 'Variegata'; ● three plants.

IVY
Hedera helix 'Kolibri' has splashed silver leaves; four ● plants.

Terracotta window box; 23cm (9in) deep, ● *55cm (22in) long.*

Height 60cm (24in)

CACTUS AND CLIVIA

✷ BRIGHT SHADE   ⚏ MEDIUM-RICH POTTING MIX   ⬱ DRY CONDITIONS

CACTUS AND CLIVIA are among a host of tender plants that simply will not survive outside in frost, but can tolerate low temperatures if they are kept in a garden room or conservatory. Indeed, I have found that many tropical plants will thrive under these conditions provided that they are kept dry in colder spells until early spring, when they begin to grow again. A bright, but not sunny, window-ledge that receives early morning or late afternoon sun is best for these pots, and in summer they can stand outside in a sheltered site.

◆ GROWING TIPS ◆

Plant up both pots when indoor light levels are naturally good. Feed with a small quantity of liquid fertilizer to encourage flowering.

Grow in the same pot for several years; clivias flower best if their roots are confined.

CACTUS •
Nopalxochia phyllanthoides has pink flowers held on glossy green stems; one plant.

CLIVIA •
Clivia miniata bears several orange flowers on each stem in spring;
two plants.

• *Stakes support flowering stems and encourage upright growth.*

Dark blue glazed pot; • 25cm (10in) deep, 30cm (12in) wide.

Height
85cm
(34in)

Exotic Orchids

✴ BRIGHT SHADE 🌡 ORCHID POTTING MIX ⚗ MOIST CONDITIONS

Here are two orchids that are relatively simple to grow indoors: one with delicate sprays of tiny flowers, and the other with larger beautifully marked flowers in subdued purples and pinks – the type that spring to the mind's eye when the name orchid is mentioned. Once their flowers have finished, and they last a long time, their strap-shaped evergreen leaves continue to make an attractive feature. During the summer months, stand both baskets of orchids in a shady position in the garden.

◆ Growing Tips ◆
Plant up at any time of year, using a ready prepared orchid potting mix or your own mix made from two parts shredded bark to one part sphagnum moss. Water regularly and feed with a weak solution of fertilizer, little and often throughout the summer.

Slipper Orchid
Paphiopedilum 'King Arthur'. Repot annually for best results;
● *two plants.*

Epiphytic Orchid ●
Phalaenopsis equestris has delicate pink flowers. Repot every three years; one plant.

Glossy dark green leaves. ●

Small wire basket; 25cm (10in) deep, 25cm (10in) wide. ●

● *Wire basket; 35cm (14in) deep, 35cm (14in) wide.*

Orchid potting mix, though well-drained, should not be allowed to dry out. ●

● *Sphagnum moss hides the plastic lining perforated with drainage holes.*

Height 42cm (17in)

SHELTERED COURTYARDS

SPACE SAVERS (*Left*)
In autumn, a trellis framework on a sheltered wall is imaginatively hung with Boston and maidenhair ferns and vivid scarlet cyclamen.

TABLE-TOP FEATURE (*Right*)
A garden table in a city courtyard is set with miniature rhododendrons, arum lilies, primulas, and saxifrages. (See pp. 40-41 for details.)

SHADY RETREAT (*Below Left*)
Bright cerise-coloured fuchsias and variegated euphorbia foliage grow particularly well in a striped tub in a shady site until the first frosts.

ENCHANTED GARDEN (*Below Right*)
Throughout summer, a magical corner is home to a statue that peers out from behind pots of hebe, hydrangea, and busy Lizzie.

COMPOSITION IN PINK

☀ SEMI-SHADE 🍴 MEDIUM-RICH, ACID, AND ALKALINE POTTING MIXES 🥄 MOIST CONDITIONS

B Y GROUPING TOGETHER different plants in their own terracotta pots, you can satisfy each plant's needs while bringing together a diverse and attractive mix of colours and shapes that you would not normally see growing side by side. The miniature rhododendron prefers well-drained acid soil, and the saxifrages require a gritty alkaline potting mix. Both will survive temperate winters in a sheltered courtyard. The pink lilies and primulas, on the other hand, enjoy a medium-rich potting mix, and are frost tender; keep them indoors over winter for protection. In late spring, all these relatively small-growing plants are at their best and make a perfect group for a low garden table.

MOSSY SAXIFRAGE •
Saxifraga 'Appleblossom'
produces masses of pink flowers;
Saxifraga 'Four Winds'
(far right) has cerise flowers;
one plant per pot.

Dense hummock of •
deeply divided leaves has
a moss-like appearance.

◆ GROWING TIPS ◆

Plant up all the pots in autumn in the appropriate potting mix. *Primula obconica* is perennial but it performs best in pots if grown for one season only. During frost bring the arums and primulas indoors for protection.

MINIATURE RHODODENDRON
*Rhododendron mackii is hardy,
and bears ice-pink flowers set
off by dark evergreen foliage;*
● one shrub.

● **ARUM LILY**
*Zantedeschia
rehmannii bears
flowers ranging in
colour from pink
to wine red, for
three months;*
three plants.

● *Tapering mid-
green leaves are
sometimes flecked
with silvery white,
and are generally
pest free.*

*Large terracotta pot;
12.5cm (5in) deep,
● 12.5cm (5in) wide.*

● **PRIMULA**
*Primula obconica has
multi-headed pink, red,
or white flowers. The
leaves can cause skin
allergies so take care;*
one plant.

Small terracotta pot; ●
*10cm (4in) deep,
10cm (4in) wide.*

Height
48cm
(19in)

Grape Hyacinths and Narcissi

✲ BRIGHT SHADE · MEDIUM-RICH POTTING MIX · MOIST CONDITIONS

Bright yellow narcissi and vivid blue grape hyacinths possess the colours and fragrances that epitomize spring. They grow easily from bulbs and I like to plant them as a pair in terracotta containers close to the house. For perfume, they are both winners. The grape hyacinths have a buttery scent while the 'Trevithian' narcissi have an almost tropical fragrance, which is even stronger than that of the jonquil, its parent. When these gems are in full flower, I position them next to a garden seat so that on warm spring days I can inhale their lovely perfume.

◆ Growing Tips ◆

Plant up both the narcissus and grape hyacinth bulbs in autumn to flower the following spring. Place the pots in a bright site. After flowering, dig up the bulbs and plant them out in the garden, where they will soon naturalize.

Narcissus ◆ *Narcissus* 'Trevithian' *has fragrant, clear sunny yellow flowers*; 50 bulbs.

Grape Hyacinth *Muscari armeniacum* 'Blue Spike' *has a short stem, double flowers, and a buttery scent*; 50 bulbs. ◆

◆ *Terracotta pot; 30cm (12in) deep, 30cm (12in) wide, painted with yoghurt to encourage moss.*

◆ *Terracotta basin; 30cm (12in) deep, 85cm (34in) wide.*

Height 85cm (34in)

FRAGRANT LILAC TREE

☀ SUN   🍴 MEDIUM-RICH POTTING MIX   ⚱ DRY CONDITIONS

ALONG WITH SWEET PEAS, lilacs produce one of the greatest flower perfumes, and this miniature lilac is no exception. It has that true lilac fragrance, with a hint of wisteria and violets in its mix. Each year, in late spring, it produces a profusion of long-lasting lavender-pink spires. 'Palibin' is ideal for growing in a pot, as it will not exceed a height of 1.5m (5ft) – a good choice for small-scale gardens that are too compact to accommodate the larger types of lilacs available.

◆ GROWING TIPS ◆

Plant up the miniature lilac tree in autumn. With good drainage and an occasional summer feeding, this low-growing species should be happy in its terracotta pot for several years. Remove flowers from newly planted lilacs and deadhead for the first few years. Prune just after flowering.

• Cut out weak shoots in winter to achieve a bushy-shaped planting.

MINIATURE LILAC •
*Syringa meyeri 'Palibin'
is hardy and produces
fragrant lilac-pink flowers
in late spring and during
early summer; one tree.*

IVY-LEAVED TOADFLAX •
*Cymbalaria muralis 'Globosa
Rosea' has pale pink flowers
and bright green kidney-shaped
leaves. It will thrive for several
years within the confines of
a container; nine plants.*

Height
85cm
(34in)

• Terracotta pot;
30cm (12in) deep,
45cm (18in) wide.

DECORATIVE DOORWAYS

FRAGRANT VERBENA JAR *(Left)*
Verbena *'Sissinghurst'* and trailing ivy-
leaved Pelargonium *'Rouletta'* introduce
colour and fragrance to a sunny doorway.

BEGONIA BASKET *(Right)*
A hanging basket of red, pink, and white
begonias brings a show of colour to a shady
entrance from summer until the first frosts.

SPRING WELCOME *(Below Left)*
Open the door to a fresh, seasonal bulb
planting of stripy purple Crocus *'Pickwick'*
and deep blue scilla. (See p. 47 for details.)

COTTAGE DOORWAY *(Below Right)*
In summer, pots of busy Lizzies in shades of
pink look very much at home sitting along-
side a mellow red brick entrance porch.

BLOSSOMING CHERRIES

☼ SUN　🖌 MEDIUM-RICH POTTING MIX　🗲 MOIST CONDITIONS

WHAT COULD BE more appropriate for a spring planting than a mix of miniature cherry trees covered in blossom, sweet-scented yellow primroses, and pale blue grape hyacinths. Contrary to popular belief, most trees can be planted in pots and, if they are potted on into increasingly larger containers, they will grow to a good size – though perhaps not quite as large as trees grown in open ground. A sunny wall against the house is the most suitable location; if you opt for a more exposed site, remember to stake the trees. (*See p.150 for details.*)

◆ GROWING TIPS ◆

Plant up the cherry trees, grape hyacinth bulbs, and primrose plants in early autumn. After flowering, cut back the shoots of the cherry trees close to the top of each tree trunk. Remove the primroses and grape hyacinths and plant them out in the garden. In their place, plant summer-flowering annuals or ivy, which will last throughout the year.

CHERRY ●
Prunus triloba bears masses of double, pale pink blossoms during mid-spring; one tree per pot.

GRAPE HYACINTH ●
Muscari azureum carries long-lasting pale blue flowers; 25 bulbs per pot.

● *Prunus triloba has a dense, twiggy habit. It can grow to a height and spread of 3m (10ft).*

● **PRIMROSE**
Primula vulgaris. After flowering, plant out this clump-forming perennial in the garden where it will naturalize; six plants per pot.

Height
1.4m
(4ft 7in)

● *Blue lime-washed terracotta pot; 38cm (15in) deep, 42cm (17in) wide.*

HARBINGERS OF SPRING

☀ SUN 🌱 MEDIUM-RICH POTTING MIX 🌢 MOIST CONDITIONS

THE EARLIEST SPRING-FLOWERING BULBS are always a cheering sight, announcing that winter is drawing to a close. Often, there can be more bad weather to come, but somehow, once these bulbs start to flower, the promise of warmer days is real. It is always worth planting spring bulbs, such as crocus and scilla, *en masse*. What's more, if you buy them in bulk they are not too expensive. Even though crocuses and scillas are remarkably hardy plants, these low plantings grow best in a sheltered spot. The scillas flower continuously for more than a month, but crocus flowers last only a few weeks.

◆ GROWING TIPS ◆

In autumn, plant up the low pans so that each bulb is close to the next. The containers must have good-sized drainage holes to prevent the bulbs becoming waterlogged and rotting. Place the containers in a sheltered site through the winter, and keep the plantings moist. After flowering, plant the bulbs out into the garden; Pickwick crocuses naturalize in grass.

CROCUS
Crocus vernus 'Pickwick'. Each bulb produces two or three flowers that last for about three weeks; 50 bulbs per pan.

SCILLA
Scilla siberica 'Atrocoerulea'. These miniatures carry intense blue flowers throughout early spring; 50 bulbs per pan.

Shallow stone pan; 10cm (4in) deep, 50cm (20in) wide.

Height
25cm
(10in)

SPRING ALPINE TROUGH

☀ SUN   🔱 MEDIUM-RICH POTTING MIX WITH GRAVEL   ⬱ DRY CONDITIONS

WHEN WINTER SNOWS on mountain slopes are melted by the warm sun, many alpine plants growing in rocky crevices burst into flower. Capture the essence of a rocky alpine landscape by planting up a trough with alpine species. If you don't have a genuine stone trough, you can buy one that is made from reconstituted stone or use an old porcelain sink. Saxifrages, phlox, and stonecrops with their sprays of pink flowers, all grow well in simulated scree conditions and look their best in late spring. Place the weathered stone trough on a paved area in an open site, where it can be seen to full advantage.

HOUSELEEK
Sempervivum 'Commander
Hay' *bears purplish rosettes*
of leaves. In summer,
the centre produces
a stem of flowers;
three plants. ●

Fine-grain gravel
is added to medium-
rich potting mix to
• aid drainage.

STONECROP
Sedum spathulifolium 'Purpureum'
is an evergreen species with fleshy
• *purple leaves;* three plants.

◆ GROWING TIPS ◆

Good drainage is essential when
growing alpines. Make sure that your
trough has a drainage hole situated at
its lowest point. Cover this with a
few crocks to prevent it becoming
blocked with soil. Using an equal
mixture of medium-rich potting mix
and fine-grain gravel, plant up the
trough in autumn or early spring, in
a bright sunny situation. Once the
saxifrages have finished flowering,
replace them with other flowering
plants, such as miniature poppies
and erodiums, for continued interest.

SAXIFRAGE
Saxifraga 'Southside
Seedling' *grows well
in rocky crevices;*
• three plants.

PHLOX
Phlox adsurgens 'Wagon Wheel'
*is a perennial species that flowers for
two months during late spring and
summer;* one plant.

• *Weathered stone trough;*
20cm (8in) deep,
70cm (28in) long.

Height
54cm
(21½in)

AZALEAS AND AJUGA

☀ SEMI-SHADE 🛠 ACID POTTING MIX ✺ MOIST CONDITIONS

AZALEAS OFFER AN ENORMOUS RANGE of flower colours, from clear blue, lilac, and purple, to brilliant orange, as well as a gamut of pastel shades. What is more, many of the deciduous varieties, including this glorious orange 'Gloria Mundi', have a rich nutmeg scent, and colourful red autumn foliage provides a second season of interest. In striking contrast, the delicate violet-flowered ajugas weave an evergreen carpet around the base of the fiery azaleas. Place the pots in a sheltered position where they will be well protected from wind and cold.

◆ GROWING TIPS ◆

Azaleas should be planted in early spring to give the plants enough time to become established before the onset of colder winter weather. Unlike other members of the large rhododendron genus, they tolerate sunshine. Water regularly, and feed occasionally during the summer.

AZALEA
Rhododendron 'Gloria Mundi'
grows to a height of 1.5m (5ft)
and has scented orange flowers;
● *one shrub per pot.*

Shallow roots make
azaleas easy to
transplant, but
they should never be
allowed to dry out. ●

● **AJUGA**
Ajuga reptans
'Atropurpurea'.
In the past its purple
flowers and leaves were
used to treat jaundice;
six plants per pot.

● *Square, well-worn*
terracotta pot,
40cm (16in) deep,
40cm (16in) wide.

Height
1m
(3ft)

TULIP BLAZE

☀ SUN/SHADE ⚒ MEDIUM-RICH POTTING MIX ⬱ MOIST CONDITIONS

F EW PLANTINGS ARE MORE striking than a large terracotta pot brimming with richly scented scarlet tulips. With very little effort on your part, they make a colourful statement and their perfume carries well. At the beginning of spring, their petals are closed tight, but they soon begin to open out, revealing their dark centres. Most spring-flowering bulbs are hardy, but they prefer bright situations. I have planted these tulips on my terrace, where they get plenty of light but not much sunshine. When I look out of my kitchen window, the splash of colour is a cheering sight on even the greyest of days.

Tulips, originally from Turkey, have been popular in Europe for the last 300 years.

TULIP •
Tulipa 'De Wet' has bright red flowers with a rich scent. Deadhead blooms when the first petals fall; 50 bulbs.

Planting bulbs in autumn gives tulips time to develop a strong root system before the cold weather sets in.

◆ GROWING TIPS ◆

Plant tulip bulbs in autumn. If the pot is very large, fill up the base with broken-up pieces of polystyrene. Then fill the container with potting mix and firm the soil to within 20cm (8in) of the rim. Arrange a layer of bulbs on the soil surface, then add potting mix, firming as you go, until the pot is filled to within 5cm (2in) of its rim. Keep the soil moist during winter, and support the stems with stakes as they grow. After flowering, cut back the stems and transplant the bulbs out into the garden.

• *Swag-motif terracotta pot; 70cm (28in) deep, 55cm (22in) wide.*

Height
1m
(3ft)

SUMMER

Summer has arrived, and as the days lengthen there is an outpouring of colour and scent. The garden is awash with flowering plants and shrubs, and in the early morning the air shimmers with the promise of warmth. This is the time of year for outdoor living, and the pleasure of idling away the hours sitting on the patio talking and eating is even greater when you are surrounded by glorious pots of fragrant plants. Even if you don't have a garden, you can still capture the heady scents of summer by growing a mixture of flowers and foliage in a window box.

❧❧

SUNNY WINDOW BOX
Creamy yellow osteospermum flowers grow up towards the sunlight, while trails of soft pink ivy pelargonium flowers, ivy, and variegated tradescantia foliage spill over the edges of this white wooden window box. (See p.75 for details.)

SUMMER GOLDS

☀ SUN/SEMI-SHADE   🖌 MEDIUM-RICH POTTING MIX   🪣 MOIST CONDITIONS

A SUNNY MIX OF YELLOW, cream, and silver flowers and foliage spills out to create this sparkling window box display. Golden marigolds and lemon-yellow petunias with their bold flowerheads form the focus of the arrangement, while feathery sedum and spiky lutea foliage add textural interest. A pair of these window boxes sits on the two sunny window-ledges outside my dining room, echoing the warm yellow and cream colour theme within. The window boxes continue to look fantastic throughout the summer and into autumn.

AFRICAN MARIGOLD ●
Tagetes erecta is a fast-growing annual. For optimum flowering deadhead regularly; three plants.

Fluted terracotta window box; 20cm (8in) deep, 78cm (31in) long. ●

Height
49cm
(19in)

PETUNIA
Petunia x *hybrida has small
lemon-yellow flowers that are
less easily damaged by rain than
those of grandiflora hybrids;
four plants.* •

SEDUM
*Sedum lineare does
well in summer but
is not hardy enough
to survive frost;
three plants.* •

◆ GROWING TIPS ◆

Plant up the terracotta window box
in spring when the chance of frost
has passed. Deadhead marigolds and
petunias frequently to encourage a
succession of flowers throughout the
summer months. Cut back petunia
stems when they start to get leggy
and they will soon produce new
flowering shoots. Watch out
for aphids: they tend to
attack young petunia plants.

LUTEA
*Monopsis lutea has a
trailing habit, which
softens the edges of
the window box;*
• *three plants.*

A PROFUSION OF PINKS

☀ SUN/SEMI-SHADE 🔱 MEDIUM-RICH POTTING MIX ⚱ MOIST CONDITIONS

SHADES OF PINK and a touch of bright white are combined to create this delicate colour mix. Vivid pink ivy-leaved pelargoniums form the centre-piece of the hanging basket, while soft, feathery upright plumes of pale pink diascia play a strong supporting role. Fronds of purple-pink verbena, tuffets of pink lobelia, and delicate white reinwardtia flowers are threaded through the edges and base of the basket, to create a frothy, natural arrangement.

◆ GROWING TIPS ◆

Plant up the basket in early summer. Position pelargoniums, diascia, and verbena in the centre of the basket and the lobelia and reinwardtia at the sides. (*See p.149.*) Feed weekly with a high potash content plant food. Water and deadhead regularly, and cut back straggly verbena stems.

PHLOX
Phlox drummondii Beauty Series *produces clusters of star-shaped flowers from summer to early autumn;* two plants.

DIASCIA ●
Diascia vigilis also makes an attractive border plant and grows well on sunny banks; two plants.

VERBENA
Verbena canadensis. As with many plants, the paler colours, especially pinks and whites, have the strongest fragrance; two plants.

IVY-LEAVED ●
PELARGONIUM
Pelargonium peltatum 'Madame Crousse' *is a good choice for a hanging basket as it produces trailing stems up to 1m (3ft) long;* three plants.

REINWARDTIA ●
Reinwardtia trigyna is frost tender; three plants.

● *Wire basket; 15cm (6in) deep, 40cm (16in) wide.*

LOBELIA ●
Lobelia pendula 'Lilac Cascade' three plants.

Height 80cm (32in)

SHIMMERING SILVER AND VIOLET

☀ SUN/SEMI-SHADE 🪴 MEDIUM-RICH POTTING MIX ⚱ MOIST CONDITIONS

VIOLETS AND PANSIES are ideal candidates for hanging baskets because they grow rapidly to form a mound of green leaves surmounted by a continuous show of flowers. Here, lilac-coloured horned violets are mixed with soft yellow and white pansies to create a subtle colour note. The effect is enhanced by a cascade of silver plectranthus foliage and trailing helichrysum. Hang the basket in a bright position, but out of direct sunlight, and it will perform well through the summer.

◆ **GROWING TIPS** ◆
Plant up the hanging basket after the chance of frost has passed. Deadhead the pansies regularly, and cut back long straggly stems. Feed the plants weekly, and protect pansies and violets from slug attack.

PANSY
Viola x *wittrockiana* 'Antique Shades' has small lemon-yellow, pink, lavender, or pale peach flowers; three plants.

HORNED VIOLET
Viola cornuta 'Lilacina' produces a mass of fragrant flowers over several months; two plants.

PANSY
Viola x *wittrockiana* 'Paper White' has exquisite white flowers with a bright yellow centre; two plants.

PLECTRANTHUS
Plectranthus coleoides 'Variegatus' is a frost-tender perennial with aromatic sage-scented silver leaves; three plants.

HELICHRYSUM
Helichrysum petiolare. A useful trailing plant for hanging baskets; three plants.

Height 70cm (28in)

Wire basket; 15cm (6in) deep, 40cm (16in) wide.

FLOWER-FILLED BORDERS

ON A PEDESTAL (Left)
A stone urn sits on a pedestal above a box-edged flowerbed. Here, pink pelargoniums, trailing white lobelia, and silver helichrysum produce a shimmering effect against a dark green backdrop of clipped yew hedges.

SILVER AND BLUE HUES (Right)
In summer, indigo-blue larkspur, filigrees of senecio, and trails of helichrysum foliage will grow prolifically in terracotta pots. This movable feast brings interest to a flower-free space in a border. (See p.60 for details.)

COLOURFUL FILLERS (Below)
A narrow border in front of a clematis-covered wall is treated to a brilliant colour planting of scarlet dahlias and a jumble of lilac campanula in beautifully weathered terracotta pots. (See pp.62-63 for details.)

SEA OF BLUE LARKSPUR

☀ SUN　🪴 MEDIUM-RICH POTTING MIX　🪣 MOIST CONDITIONS

TRUE BLUE FLOWERS such as larkspur, plumbago, hydrangeas, and gentians are not commonplace but they can play a very special part in container gardening. Here vivid blue larkspur is set against the silver plumes of *Senecio maritima* 'Silver Dust' and the delicate, trailing leaves of *Helichrysum petiolare*. This silver mix of foliage seems to intensify the rich blue hue of the larkspur flowers. Stand the terracotta pot in the middle of an herbaceous border or use it to add extra interest to a paved area.

◆ GROWING TIPS ◆

In cold regions where late frosts are likely, delay planting up the pot until mid-spring because helichrysum and senecio cannot tolerate frost. Larkspur is hardy, but not long-lasting.

LARKSPUR
Delphinium consolida 'Blue Cloud' is a hardy dwarf variety; four plants.

SENECIO ●
Senecio maritima 'Silver Dust' has yellow flowers; Remove them to encourage bushy foliage; three plants.

Terracotta pot; ●
40cm (16in) deep,
45cm (18in) wide.

● HELICHRYSUM
Helichrysum petiolare has grey-felted leaves, and is grown as an annual; three plants.

Height
85cm
(34in)

PINK MIST

☀ SUN/SEMI-SHADE 🖌 MEDIUM-RICH POTTING MIX ☕ MOIST CONDITIONS

W HEN PLANNING SUMMER COLOUR, don't rely just on annuals: take a longer-term view. There are many beautiful perennials that produce a wealth of flowers over the summer months. This planting of scabious and erigeron bears rich pink flowers from early summer to autumn, and will continue to thrive in the same container for two or three years, needing very little maintenance. The cauldron-like shape of the large terracotta pot is ideally suited to the low-growing habit of scabious and erigeron plants. I've used trails of ivy to spill over and soften the container's edges.
Place this planting on the edge of an herbaceous border.

◆ GROWING TIPS ◆

Plant up these hardy species in early spring. To prevent the fast-growing ivies taking over the entire pot in the second season, thin out their roots and fill in the holes with potting mix.

Allow several of the scabious flowers to go to seed. Seedheads make an attractive addition to the display.

SCABIOUS
Scabiosa caucasica 'Pink Mist' bears rich pink flowers; three plants.

IVY
Hedera helix 'Gavotte' carries small, elongated, dark green leaves; four plants.

ERIGERON
Erigeron 'Charity' has a low-growing, spreading habit; three plants.

Terracotta cauldron; 38cm (15in) deep, 25cm (10in) wide.

Height
75cm
(30in)

REGAL MIX

☼ SUN ⚒ MEDIUM-RICH POTTING MIX ⚲ MOIST CONDITIONS

SMALL-GROWING DAHLIAS have great appeal: they are available in a staggering range of colours; they flower later than many other summer plants; and, unlike the giant-flowered varieties, they don't require staking. Here dahlias are teamed up with *Campanula poscharskyana*, a long-lived hardy perennial that seeds itself freely and enjoys growing in cracks and crevices in walls and paths. Luckily, this campanula also thrives in pots, and produces several flushes of flowers from early summer until the first frosts in autumn.

CAMPANULA ◆
Campanula poscharskyana spreads quickly. Its bell-shaped violet flowers soon pour over the sides of the container; four plants per pot.

◆ GROWING TIPS ◆

Plant dahlias and campanula in pots in early summer. To keep dahlias bushy, take out tall growing tips and, once in bloom, deadhead regularly to reward yourself with a continual show of red flowers. After the first flush of campanula flowers, trim back the plants to encourage more flowering stems. Watch out for earwigs, which love to eat dahlias.

Terracotta pot; ◆ 45cm (18in) deep, 50cm (20in) wide.

Height
85cm
(34in)

DAHLIA
*Dahlia 'Sunny Red' is
rewarding for both its intense
colour and prolific flowering;*
three plants per pot. •

*Dahlias also make excellent cut
flowers and bloom continuously
throughout summer.* •

*Campanula also
grows well between
the stones and bricks
in old walls.* •

Terracotta pots •
*kept outdoors all year
must be frost-proof or
they will crack and flake.*

POOLSIDE PLANTINGS

DAPPLED SHADE (*Left*)
A Chinese glazed hexagonal pot spilling over with lilac-coloured lobelia, blue phacelia, and silver helichrysum, sits beside a terracotta pan of pratia displaying a delicate mound of blue star-shaped flowers. On the edge of a small pool overgrown with duckweed, these container plantings make a tranquil focal point for a shady retreat. (See p.66 for details.)

PURPLE HAZE (*Right*)
A selection of pots and urns brimming with rich purple campanula, deep red dianthus, and pink pelargoniums is arranged on a number of different levels to add interest to this informal paved pool area. The pool itself is filled with tall-growing, leafy iris plants.

SIMPLE BEAUTY (*Above*)
White fibrous-rooted begonias in a square wooden trough enjoy the humidity of a watery location. Set against a backdrop of large water lily leaves, this planting looks all the better for its simplicity. (See pp.68-69 for details.)

SENSORY DELIGHT (*Right*)
At the edge of the pool, an old lead trough overflowing with bright pink pelargoniums and scented verbena combines with the sound of splashing water from an attractive shell-shaped fountain, to delight the senses.

COOL BLUES

☼ SEMI-SHADE   🌱 MEDIUM-RICH POTTING MIX   ⚱ MOIST CONDITIONS

PHACELIA WITH ITS DELICATE azure-blue flowers, a froth of lilac lobelia, and trails of silver-grey helichrysum create a distinctly cool combination. Phacelia is an unusual choice but well worth remembering when you consider the lack of true blue-coloured flowers available. Lobelia, on the other hand, is a very popular trailing plant as it grows quickly, filling out the display. Available in clear, pale, and deep blues, purples, lilacs, and pinks, lobelia produces a mass of flowers for months on end. To show off this low-level planting to best advantage, place it in a shady poolside location.

◆ GROWING TIPS ◆

Plant up the pot in early summer. Water regularly to keep the potting mix moist, and feed at least once a week. Phacelia can be cut back after its first flowering, and will produce a second crop of flowers. Trim the helichrysum stems periodically to prevent the foliage becoming too long and straggly.

LOBELIA
Lobelia erinus spreads rapidly, and blooms until the first frosts;
• *five plants.*

PHACELIA
Phacelia campanularia carries deep blue flowers, from early to late summer, that are attractive to bees;
four plants.

Phacelia • leaves are fragrant when crushed.

HELICHRYSUM
Helichrysum petiolare is an evergreen shrub. Remove creamy yellow flowers to encourage healthy, bushy foliage;
four plants.

Height
60cm
(24in)

Hexagonal glazed pot; 45cm (18in) deep, 60cm (24in) wide.

CORAL AND JADE

☼ BRIGHT SHADE 🔨 MEDIUM-RICH POTTING MIX ⚱ MOIST CONDITIONS

OFTEN THE SIMPLEST of plantings can give the greatest joy. Here busy Lizzie – a celebrated container plant – is paired with miniature bamboo grass to great effect in terms of colour and texture. This New Guinea hybrid with its coral-coloured flowers has only recently become available at garden centres, and is distinguished from other types by the crystalline sheen on its petals and larger leaf size. Colours range from cyclamen-pink and bright orange to subtle shades of lilac and salmon-pink. Both busy Lizzies and bamboo enjoy a bright but shaded position, and look at home in a water garden.

◆ GROWING TIPS ◆

Plant up the pot after the chance of frost has passed because although New Guinea hybrids are robust, miniature bamboo grasses are frost tender. Keep the plants well watered, and feed once a fortnight so that the busy Lizzies flower continuously throughout the summer months. To avoid rot, remove dead flowerheads that drop into the planting.

BAMBOO GRASS
Pogonatherum paniceum has pink leaf tips that work well with the coral busy Lizzie flowers; three plants.

BUSY LIZZIE
Impatiens New Guinea hybrid is a robust plant with glistening coral-coloured flowers; three plants.

Height
50cm
(20in)

Green glazed pot; 30cm (12in) deep, 50cm (20in) wide.

SHADE-LOVING COMPANIONS

☀ BRIGHT SHADE   ⚒ MEDIUM-RICH POTTING MIX   ⚑ MOIST CONDITIONS

F EW FLOWERING PLANTS actually enjoy growing in shade, but these are two that will flourish. Variegated-leaved zebrinas are usually grown indoors, but they will do terrifically well outside in containers and hanging baskets, if they are given a warm, sheltered location. The zebrina leaves are evergreen and last throughout the summer and autumn months. To encourage a continuous show of white blooms from the small-flowered begonia, place this pair of wooden troughs in bright shade, beside a water feature where they can benefit from the humidity.

◆ GROWING TIPS ◆

Plant up the troughs after the chance of frost has passed. Feed the zebrina and begonia plants once a fortnight to encourage healthy leaves and flowers. Keep zebrina plants bushy by pinching out the longer growing tips. Both wooden trough plantings will last throughout the summer months and until the onset of the first autumn frosts.

ZEBRINA
Zebrina pendula has fleshy stems, and is a fast-growing, trailing perennial;
six plants. ●

For indoor container plantings, grow zebrina in very bright light. Growth becomes untidy and straggly if the
● *light level is too low.*

Wooden trough; ●
23cm (9in) deep,
70cm (28in) wide.

BEGONIA
Begonia semperflorens 'Coco
Ducolor' *is one of the most
popular and reliable of
summer bedding plants;*
five plants. ●

*Purple-bronze leaves echo
the colouring of the
zebrina foliage.* ●

● *Wooden trough;
30cm (12in) deep,
45cm (18in) wide.*

Treat the wood ●
*with a clear wood
preservative. Avoid
creosote, which is
harmful to plants.*

Height
68cm
(27in)

DECKS OF DELIGHT

ALPINE BOWLS (*Left*)

A shady platform on a flight of wooden garden steps is a good spot for low bowls of alpines, such as stonecrops and houseleeks. The huge spiked leaves of gunnera introduce textural interest, while brilliant 'Red Emperor' mimulus adds a welcome dash of colour to capture your attention.

CENTRE STAGE (*Right*)

A weathered terracotta pot is filled with brilliant red nasturtiums and apricot verbena, a combination that looks particularly effective in its sunny position against the vivid green vine leaves that clamber over the rail of the deck patio. (See p.72 for details.)

BOARDWALK (*Below*)

In summer, a stepped deck leading up to a sheltered verandah provides a flower-filled platform for trumpets of sweet-scented white tobacco plants, terracotta pots of pale pink snapdragons, a hanging basket of flowering pelargoniums, and low bowls planted with busy Lizzies and shocking pink verbena.

SUN-LOVING NASTURTIUMS

☀ SUN 🍴 MEDIUM-RICH POTTING MIX 🫗 MOIST CONDITIONS

LONG-LASTING, vivid scarlet flowers combined with decorative trailing foliage make nasturtiums a very popular choice for container plantings. Here they are planted simply but effectively with pale apricot verbena, whose densely packed, lightly scented florets contrast with the bolder nasturtium flowerheads. Apricot verbena was introduced fairly recently and has a subtle perfume allied to apricots. If you cannot find this special variety at garden centres, use a pink verbena, such as 'Silver Ann', instead.

◆ GROWING TIPS ◆

Plant up the pot in early summer. Check the nasturtium leaves and flowers periodically for black fly infestation, and spray them with a mixture of water and washing-up liquid. Verbenas are susceptible to mildew so, when watering, ensure that the soil is moist but not soggy.

Nasturtiums will flower profusely ● without feeding.

NASTURTIUM ●
Tropaeolum majus 'Empress of India' is a sun-loving, fast-growing, fully hardy annual; five plants.

● **VERBENA**
Verbena x hybrida bears primrose-like flowers arranged in large clusters; four plants.

*Pastryware terracotta pot; ●
30cm (12in) deep,
38cm (15in) wide.*

Height
70cm
(28in)

BED OF MARIGOLDS

☀ SUN 🖌 MEDIUM-RICH POTTING MIX 🏺 MOIST CONDITIONS

A GOLDEN BED OF AFRICAN MARIGOLDS, blanket flowers, and coleus is shown off to best advantage in this low-level wooden trough. I've planted burnt orange-coloured African marigolds and blanket flowers in rows at opposite ends of the container, and added gold- and lime-green-coloured coleus to sit between the two. As a rule, planting in straight rows should be avoided, but in this display it helps to distinguish between flower types that share similar colourways. For maximum impact, site this predominantly orange planting near deep red or yellow flowers and foliage in the garden. Hot colours such as these can also look interesting adjacent to pale pink flowers.

◆ GROWING TIPS ◆

Plant up the trough in mild weather towards the end of spring. Deadhead marigolds and blanket flowers regularly to encourage them to produce even more flowers. To achieve the best green and gold leaf colour from the coleus plants, remove flower spikes, and take out longer growing shoots to keep the plants bushy. Feed the display at least once every two weeks.

BLANKET FLOWER
Gaillardia x grandiflora 'Dazzler'
has daisy-like red flowers that last
for several months; five plants. ●

COLEUS
Coleus blumei is grown for
its attractive green and gold
leaves; three plants. ●

Height
53cm
(21in)

AFRICAN MARIGOLD
Tagetes erecta grows
well in an open site;
eight plants. ●

● *Wooden trough;*
20cm (8in) deep,
74cm (29in) wide.

TRAILING CONVOLVULUS

☀ SUN 🌱 MEDIUM-RICH POTTING MIX ⚒ MOIST CONDITIONS

CONVOLVULUS, WITH A MASS of vibrant purple-blue flowers,
is a good choice for container gardeners because, with just
three plants, you can create a full display. This actual planting
has survived in my London garden for four years, and each year
produces a very impressive show of flowers. In my experience,
Convolvulus sabatius is the most reliable plant of the convolvulus
family for growing in containers; *Convolvulus tricolor* tends to
become straggly, and *Convolvulus althaeoides* simply does not
grow well in pots. Position this planting on a deck or paved
area where it can be viewed in
all its glory.

◆ GROWING TIPS ◆

Plant up the container in spring. Cut
back all the flowers after their first
flush. For best results, feed the display
once a fortnight with a liquid tomato
plant food. Pests do not seem to be a
problem. Convolvulus can withstand
a few degrees of frost, but shelter the
planting from severe cold in winter.

CONVOLVULUS
*Convolvulus sabatius flowers
in summer and early autumn;*
● three plants.

*The flowers open up
each morning and
close again
in the early
evening.* ●

Leaf display ●
*continues until
late autumn.*

● *Terracotta pot;
34cm (13in) deep,
40cm (16in) wide.*

Height
55cm
(22in)

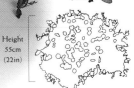

PASTEL PALETTE

☀ SUN   ⚗ MEDIUM-RICH POTTING MIX   ⚱ MOIST CONDITIONS

COLOUR PLAYS an important part in this planting. Rich creamy yellow osteospermum flowers are juxtaposed with brilliant pink pelargoniums, the colours of which are subtly picked up by green-, pink-, and white-striped tradescantia leaves. I was once told that mixing yellow and pink is a great sin, in which case I am a great sinner, for I love to pair up these pastel colours. This mix, grown in a sunny position on a deck, terrace, or patio, will look fresh and sunny through the summer months.

◆ GROWING TIPS ◆

Plant up the display in early summer. To encourage the maximum number of new flowers, deadhead both the pelargoniums and osteospermum on a regular basis. Whereas pelargoniums produce an unending show of colour, osteospermums produce three waves of blooms throughout the summer.

OSTEOSPERMUM
Osteospermum 'Buttermilk' has aromatic grey-green leaves; three plants. ●

IVY-LEAVED PELARGONIUM
Pelargonium peltatum 'Crocodile'; three plants. ●

TRADESCANTIA
Tradescantia fluminensis 'Albovittata' is an attractive frost-tender evergreen; three plants. ●

An upright habit is characteristic of this ● semi-woody plant.

● White wooden window box; 30cm (12in) deep, 60cm (24in) wide.

Height 68cm (27in)

PAVED PATIOS

HERB SELECTION (*Far Left*)
A sunny south-facing wall is a perfect site for growing herbs. Here, a vegetable rack lined with moss makes an interesting three-tier planter. (See pp.78-79 for details.)

MIX AND MATCH (*Left*)
An eclectic mix of plant shapes is brought together in this attractive grouping of pots. The display includes fleshy-leaved succulents, marguerites, pelargoniums, and a cordyline with its fountain of dark coppery leaves.

COPPER CAULDRON (*Below Left*)
A copper tub, left to stand, will develop a delicious blue-green patina, and looks superb planted with lilac petunias, feathery purple heliotrope, pink diascia, and cat mint.

LILAC URN (*Below Right*)
Fragrant lilac heliotrope and the mauve-blue daisies of felicia are perfectly matched in an elegant classical-shaped terracotta urn.

AROMATIC HERB RACK

☀ SUN   🪣 MEDIUM-RICH POTTING MIX   🖤 MOIST CONDITIONS

A MULTI-STOREY CONTAINER is ideal for housing a selection of culinary herbs in a small garden, as you can grow three times as many plants as usual in a restricted space. I have made the planting decorative as well as practical by including scented pelargoniums (their leaves can be used to flavour ice-cream or syllabub) among the more traditional culinary herbs: parsley, sage, thyme, basil, chives, and marjoram. Many of these popular herbs have a Mediterranean origin, and are therefore sun-loving. A sunny paved area outside the kitchen door makes a perfect location for this aromatic herb rack.

◆ GROWING TIPS ◆

Plant up the herbs in spring, in a tall wire rack that allows good drainage. Line each pocket of the rack with moss and heavy duty plastic. Pierce plenty of holes for drainage in the plastic and fill each pocket of the wire rack with medium-rich potting mix. The herb plantings will last for several years. If the mixed herbs in the smaller terracotta pots become too crowded, divide them in autumn.

CHIVES
Allium schoenoprasum has a mild onion flavour and carries globular mauve flowers in mid-summer; two plants. ●

OREGANO
Origanum vulgare 'Curly Gold' bears savoury flavoured leaves that scorch in ● direct sunlight; one plant.

GOLD VARIEGATED SAGE ●
Salvia officinalis 'Icterina' has a milder flavour than common sage, and is popular with bees; one plant.

LEMON THYME
Thymus x citriodorus 'Aureus' is a hardy plant, noted for its lemon-scented leaves; one plant. ●

● *Terracotta pot; 20cm (8in) deep, 12cm (5in) wide.*

Height
1m
(3ft)

DARK OPAL BASIL ●
Ocimum basilicum purpureum.
A native of India, it is often
placed on window-sills to deter
flies; four plants.

SCENTED PELARGONIUM
Pelargonium 'Letitia' *is a tender
plant and needs replacing each
● spring; one plant.*

GOLDEN THYME
Thymus 'Doone Valley' *has a
lemon scent. Pick leaves in summer
when the plant is in bloom;
one plant. ●*

THYME
*Thymus doerfleri
has aromatic silver
leaves and pale
pink flowers;*
● *two plants.*

**SCENTED
PELARGONIUM**
Pelargonium crispum
'Variegatum'. *Rub the
scented leaves to release
their tangy fragrance;
one plant. ●*

CURLED PARSLEY
*Petroselinum crispum
grows well in most
containers. Place
parsley next to rose
shrubs to improve
their health and scent;*
● *three plants.*

**SCENTED
PELARGONIUM**
*Pelargonium x fragrans
bears attractive leaves
with a spicy pine
flavour; one plant. ●*

POT MARJORAM
*Origanum onites has
dark green peppery
flavoured leaves and
small pale pink flowers;
one plant.*

● *Wire rack
lined with
green moss
and plastic;
75cm (30in)
high, 25cm
(10in) wide.*

PETUNIA BASKET

☀ SUN/SEMI-SHADE 🍴 MEDIUM-RICH POTTING MIX ⚱ MOIST CONDITIONS

SMALL CONTAINERS call for diminutive plants and flowers that will not overwhelm one another or the proportions of the pot. Here a latticework terracotta basket is filled with a vibrant mix of pink and red flowers. Coral-pink pelargoniums are teamed up with vivid red phlox, pink petunias, and rust-pink clusters of polygonum flowers, all offset by a variety of leaves. Place this eye-catching display in a bright but sheltered location.

◆ GROWING TIPS ◆

Plant up the basket in early summer. Deadhead petunias, pelargoniums, and phlox regularly to encourage new flowers, and feed the display every two weeks with a high potash content fertilizer. Take pelargonium cuttings in late summer and then overwinter them in a frost-free site.

PETUNIA
Petunia Resisto Series 'Brick'
*has particularly resilient flowers
that are undamaged by heavy
rain;* one plant.

ZONAL PELARGONIUM
Pelargonium 'Frank Headley'
*is an attractive cream- and
green-leaved variety with pink
flowers;* two plants.

POLYGONUM
Polygonum
'Victory Carpet'.
*A variety with a low,
trailing habit;*
two plants.

PHLOX
Phlox drummondii
'Fantasy Mixed'.
*A bushy annual with
pale pink flowers;*
one plant.

*Latticework basket;
25cm (10in) deep,
40cm (16in) wide.*

Height
40cm
(16in)

OASIS GARDEN

❈ BRIGHT SHADE ⬚ MEDIUM-RICH POTTING MIX AND GRIT ⬭ DRY CONDITIONS

A BOWL OF SUCCULENTS can provide a welcome oasis in your living room or kitchen, and the variety of natural forms and colours common to these evergreen plants offers year-round interest. Some succulents produce a few sparse leaves, others fleshy leaves, while some have no leaves at all. They all make excellent houseplants as they have adapted to growing in dry, inhospitable areas and therefore require very little maintenance. Succulents produce a number of babies and side shoots that you can remove from the parent and plant up in a new arrangement.

◆ GROWING TIPS ◆
Succulents are best planted in spring or summer in a mixture of equal parts medium-rich potting mix and fine grit. Keep the bowl planting on the dry side. Even in rooms with central heating, succulents require watering only once every two to three weeks. Good drainage is essential.

SENECIO
Senecio kleinii;
one plant. ●

HAWORTHIA
Haworthia attenuata 'Clariperla'
is a clump-forming succulent;
two plants. ●

ECHEVERIA
Echeveria harmsii, grows
wild from Texas south to
● *Argentina; one plant.*

CRASSULA
Crassula lycopodioides
has leafless stems
branching from its base;
one plant. ●

SENECIO
Senecio articulata bears
white or red brush-like
● *flowers; one plant.*

GASTERIA ●
Gasteria verrucosa
is an easy-to-grow,
stemless succulent;
one plant.

● *China bowl;*
12cm (5in) deep,
40cm (16in) wide.

Height
36cm
(14in)

FLOWER AND FERN DISPLAY

☀ SHADE/SEMI-SHADE 🖌 ACID POTTING MIX ⟿ MOIST CONDITIONS

FRESH GREEN FERN LEAVES marry beautifully with clear yellow begonias and lilac-blue hydrangeas in this lead planter. In an horizontal display, the shapes and textures of flowers and foliage take on great importance. Fronds of maidenhair fern and hard shield fern offset the large, smooth leaves of begonias and hydrangeas, while the compact, rose-like begonia flowerheads complement the frothy hydrangea mopheads. Position the planter in a sheltered site along the edge of a patio, next to a wall, or against a backdrop of taller ferns.

HYDRANGEA
Hydrangea macrophylla
'Générale Vicomtesse de
Vibraye' prefers a sheltered site.
An acid-based soil produces lilac-
blue bracts that flower for three
months; two plants. •

MAIDENHAIR FERN
Adiantum raddianum is the most
commonly cultivated. It likes to be
watered frequently and dislikes
direct sunlight; two plants. •

Antique lead planter; •
15cm (6in) deep,
1.2m (4ft) long.

◆ GROWING TIPS ◆

Plant up the lead container after the chance of frost has passed. During autumn, plant out the hard shield ferns and hydrangeas in the garden. Before the first autumn frosts, bring tender maidenhair ferns and begonias indoors. Stop watering the begonia plants completely so that they dry off. Carefully remove their yellow foliage and store the begonia tubers in almost-dry fibrous soil until spring when they can be planted out.

Height
63cm
(25in)

BEGONIA
Begonia x tuberhybrida 'Festiva'
is a tuberous begonia producing double
bright yellow blooms from early to late
● *summer; two plants.*

HARD SHIELD FERN
Polystichum aculeatum is
often found growing in
woodland areas by water;
three plants. ●

● *Large green*
hydrangea leaves
help to soften the
horizontal edges
of the container.

POTS FOR PERGOLAS

RUSTIC RETREAT (*Left*)
A rustic loggia bathed in afternoon sun is a perfect place to sit and admire this magnificent fuchsia 'Countess of Maritza', circled by a ruff of busy Lizzies. (See p.87 for details.)

SHADY PERGOLA (*Right*)
In an oasis of late-summer green, beneath a canopy of white, scented jasmine, stands a monumental terracotta pot of 'Ashford Red' abutilon. These bell-shaped flowers are produced for several months throughout the summer, and are echoed by the blood leaf in the small pot. (See p.86 and p.109 for details.)

CLASSICAL LOGGIA (*Below*)
Spiralled box trees in pots and half barrels planted with bay mopheads enhance the architectural beauty of this classical loggia.

TOWERING ABUTILON

☀ SUN   🌱 MEDIUM-RICH POTTING MIX   ⚒ MOIST CONDITIONS

ABUTILONS ARE REWARDING PLANTS because in a single season they grow several metres high and are covered in flowers from mid-summer until the first autumn frosts. The varieties of abutilon that do best in containers are all frost tender. *Abutilon* x *hybridum* 'Ashford Red', used in this display, carries bell-shaped salmon-red flowers, but orange, pink, yellow, and white varieties are also available. The hardiest variety, *Abutilon* x *suntense*, has lilac or white flowers and blooms in spring and early summer. The monumental scale of abutilons makes them a dramatic choice for a sunny but sheltered arbour, pergola, or loggia.

ABUTILON
Abutilon x *hybridum* *'Ashford Red' carries a profusion of bell-shaped flowers for five months;*
● three plants.

Bamboo stakes support •
growing abutilon stems.

◆ GROWING TIPS ◆
Plant up the pot after the chance of frost has passed. Prune the growing tips when the stems are about 1m (3ft) high. Stake the plants as they grow to prevent them blowing over in high winds. The lower stems of abutilon can be bare, so grow a matt-forming plant such as *Sagina glabra* 'Aurea' around the base. Throughout the growing season feed weekly, and keep the pot well watered.

Height
1.2m
(4ft)

PEARLWORT ●
Sagina glabra 'Aurea'
*produces hummocks of
gold-green foliage;*
seven plants.

● *Terracotta basin;*
35cm (14in) deep,
75cm (30in) wide.

CASCADING FUCHSIA CANOPY

☀ BRIGHT SHADE 🍴 RICH POTTING MIX ⚱ MOIST CONDITIONS

A STANDARD FUCHSIA swathed in hundreds of flowers is a
truly amazing sight. The best standards are produced
by varieties of fuchsia that have good upright
growth, such as 'Avocet', 'Falling Stars', 'New
Fascination', and 'Marin Glow'. Plant pale
pink busy Lizzie New Guinea hybrids
around the foot of the standard in
colours that echo those of the
fuchsia sepals. Busy Lizzies are
the perfect companion plants
for fuchsias because they
thrive in exactly the same
growing conditions and
cover up the bare stem of the
standard. A sheltered arbour or
loggia makes an excellent site as
most fuchsia standards dislike windy
locations and prefer bright shade.

FUCHSIA •
*Fuchsia 'Countess of Maritza'. The
drooping habit of this variety also makes it
a good choice for a hanging basket; one plant.*

◆ GROWING TIPS ◆

It is relatively straightforward to
train a standard fuchsia (*see p.151.*)
Ideally, start in autumn of the year
before you want flowers, and grow
the plant in a frost-free environment.
With strong varieties such as this,
the stem of the standard will thicken
by 7.5-10cm (3-4in) and produce a
reasonable-sized flowering head in
the first summer. Its main flowering
will be in late summer to autumn.

• BUSY LIZZIE
Impatiens New Guinea
hybrid *produces large
pinkish white flowers;
four plants.*

Height
1.5m
(5ft)

*Square, chrysanthemum-
motif terracotta pot;
40cm (16in) deep
40cm (16in) wide.* •

SUMMER STRIPES

☼ SUN/SEMI-SHADE 🛋 MEDIUM-RICH POTTING MIX ⚱ MOIST CONDITIONS

PETUNIAS AND ZONAL PELARGONIUMS both have a long and bountiful flowering season, which makes them a popular choice for summer container plantings. Here, crimson-pink-and-white-striped petunias are mixed with deep pink pelargoniums to produce a wonderfully vibrant effect. In addition, the pale silver-and-green-striped leaves of tradescantia foliage echo the pattern on the petunia petals. In the perfect position, standing guard at the entrance to an arbour or pergola, this easily grown planting makes a bold, colourful statement.

PETUNIA ●
Petunia x hybrida Star Series
flowers for up to four months;
three plants per pot.

PETUNIA ●
Petunia x hybrida
Star Series *needs full*
sun to give of its best.

Height
1m
(3ft)

◆ GROWING TIPS ◆

Plant up the pots once the chance of frost has passed. Deadhead every day to encourage the maximum number of blooms. Cut back the flowering stems half way through the growing season if the plants start to become leggy Feed every week with a high potassium content plant food.

ZONAL PELARGONIUM
Pelargonium 'Sterling Stent' is a prolific flowerer. This variety has a dark circular zone on each leaf; three plants per pot. •

TRADESCANTIA
Tradescantia fluminensis 'Quicksilver' has thin almost transparent leaves, the undersides of which appear purple in bright • *light;* three plants per pot.

• *Reconstituted stone pots; 38cm (15in) deep, 25cm (10in) wide.*

WINDOW DISPLAYS

WINDOW OF OPPORTUNITY (Far Left)
A shaded window-sill plays host to a small terracotta window box planted with yellow and orange tuberous begonias, yellow and white pansies, and pink double busy Lizzies. All these will flower throughout the summer and autumn. (See pp.94-95 for details.)

PERFECT PANSIES (Left)
In early spring, a collection of small pots filled with Universal Series white pansies, creates a welcoming display on a window-ledge.

BEHIND BARS (Below)
Bars at the window to keep intruders at bay become less of an eyesore when hidden behind a floriferous planting of swan river daisies, scaevola, and the trailing silver foliage of artemisia. (See pp.92-93 for details.)

FEATHERY FILIGREE

☀ SUN/SEMI-SHADE　🛠 MEDIUM-RICH POTTING MIX　⚱ MOIST CONDITIONS

S WAN RIVER DAISIES AND SCAEVOLA are two summer-flowering annuals
that are becoming increasingly popular. Swan river daisies have
filigrees of tiny leaves surmounted by bushy crowns of pink daisy flowers
with bright yellow centres. *Scaevola emula* produces long spikes of lilac
flowers that last until late autumn and the first frosts. They work well
together visually as the delicacy of one balances the coarseness of
the other, and luckily they enjoy the same growing conditions.
 In this planting, swan river daisy and scaevola are
joined by the hardy evergreen, *Artemisia* 'Silver
Brocade'. All three plants grow vigorously and
have a low growing habit, which makes
them a good choice for a window
box or trough. They will thrive in
the limited space of a container,
spilling over the edges to
form a full display.

ARTEMISIA ●
Artemisia 'Silver Brocade'
has abundant, aromatic,
silver-grey foliage;
two plants.

◆ GROWING TIPS ◆

Plant up the window box after the
chance of frost has passed. Don't
worry about deadheading the daisies
or scaevola, but remove the long
flowering stems of the artemisia
to encourage bushy growth.
Feed the plants fortnightly
with a high potash content
liquid plant food.

Height
64cm
(25in)

SWAN RIVER DAISY
Brachycome iberidifolia
continues to flower well
into the autumn months;
● three plants.

● SCAEVOLA
*Scaevola emula is an Australian
plant. It is a fast-growing, long-
flowering annual;* three plants.

*Artemisia is an evergreen
and so can be used to
form the foundation of
● a winter planting.*

● *Rustic wooden trough;
40cm (16in) deep,
64cm (25in) long.*

SHADY TRIO

☼ SHADE/SEMI-SHADE   🖌 MEDIUM-RICH POTTING MIX   🝰 MOIST CONDITIONS

O RANGE, PRIMROSE-YELLOW, and ice-pink flowers are brought together in this terracotta window box to produce one of my favourite colour mixes. Double-flowered busy Lizzies, pansies, and begonias make good companions and are particularly useful plants for container gardeners as they will flourish in shady sites. Busy Lizzies have been widely hybridized, and this double-flowered type produces enormous quantities of pale pink, rose-like flowers. Display this glorious planting on a sheltered window-ledge to brighten up an area that doesn't receive much direct sunlight.

PANSY ●
Viola x wittrockiana 'Antique
Shades' *comes in a range of
colours; here I've selected a
plant with pale primrose-
yellow flowers; two plants.*

*Large, serrated-edged
begonia leaves add
textural interest.* ●

◆ GROWING TIPS ◆

All the plants in the display, except pansies, are tender so in cold areas plant up the window box after the chance of frost has passed. Remove fleshy begonia flowers that drop off into the window box as they can cause 'damping off' if they lie against leaves and stems within the planting. Deadhead the pansies and cut back straggly stems to encourage substantial new flower growth.

PANSY ●
*Viola x wittrockiana
'Paper White' works
well in containers as a
filler plant or main
feature, in semi-shade or
full sun; one plant.*

BUSY LIZZIE
Impatiens Rosette Series
offers rose-like, pink flowers;
● three plants.

BEGONIA
Begonia x *tuberhybrida*
'Non-Stop Orange'.
*A variety that lives up
to its promising name;*
● three plants.

*● Griffin-patterned
terracotta window box;
20cm (8in) deep,
45cm (18in) long.*

Height
50cm
(20in)

VIBRANT VERBENA

✹ SUN 　🌱 MEDIUM-RICH POTTING MIX 　⚱ MOIST CONDITIONS

CREATE A SHIMMERING basket of scarlet and crimson by growing red verbena and phlox flowers against a dark background of red-veined polygonum leaves and trails of dark green ivy. I have chosen this variety of verbena for its subtle fragrance and for the sparkly white centres of its vivid flowers. Hanging baskets brimming with bright colour are ideal containers for livening up a bare wall, or for suspending from the horizontal beam of a garden arbour or pergola. With frequent watering and deadheading, this colourful planting will flower through the summer months.

◆ GROWING TIPS ◆

Plant up the basket in early summer. In hot weather, water the display twice a day. Feed the plants weekly with a high potash content liquid plant food, and deadhead regularly. Verbena is prone to mildew during hot, dry spells. Spray the contents of the hanging basket from time to time with fungicide to prevent infection.

PHLOX
Phlox drummondii comes in a brilliant selection of colours; four plants.

POLYGONUM
Polygonum 'Victory Carpet' also grows well in rock gardens or on banks; four plants.

Moss-filled wire basket 15cm (6in) deep, 40cm (16in) wide.

VERBENA
Verbena x hybrida 'Defiance' flowers profusely from early summer to the first frosts; five plants.

IVY
Hedera helix 'Ivalace'. A small-leaved form, suitable for indoor plantings; four plants.

Height
65cm
(26in)

SKEINS OF GOLD

☀ BRIGHT SHADE   ⚒ MEDIUM-RICH POTTING MIX   ⚱ MOIST CONDITIONS

FOR A FRESH green and yellow hanging basket throughout the summer, combine lysimachia and tradescantia foliage with bright yellow oxalis and cosmos flowers. You could also try ivies in a range of leaf colours and shapes for a similar effect; alternatively, use variegated gold and green *Vinca minor* 'Albo variegata', which has long trailing stems, or the gold and silver variegated forms of *Helichrysum petiolare*. Position this natural-looking arrangement in bright shade where lysimachia, tradescantia, and oxalis will be most at home.

◆ GROWING TIPS ◆

Plant up the hanging basket in early summer. Cut back the cosmos plants to prevent them looking too straggly. Feed the display twice a week with a high potash content plant food to encourage flowering. Water liberally to prevent the planting drying out, especially during hot sunny weather.

TRADESCANTIA ●
*Tradescantia fluminensis 'Variegata',
with its attractive striped leaves, makes
an excellent trailing plant for hanging
baskets;* four plants.

OXALIS ●
*Oxalis lobata is a dainty,
low-growing plant with
distinctive red stems;*
four plants.

● *Wire basket,
15cm (6in) deep,
40cm (16in) wide.*

Height
1m
(3ft)

LYSIMACHIA ●
*Lysimachia nummularia 'Aurea'
produces trails of golden leaves that
grow up to 2m (6ft) in length;*
three plants.

COSMOS ●
*Cosmos 'Sunny Gold'
has a long season of
flowers if deadheaded
regularly;* three plants.

PLANTS FOR PATHWAYS

WINTER BERRIES (*Left*)
In autumn, hardy wintergreen and juniper are planted in a low, tarnished copper bowl, to create a shimmering planting on a red brick path. (See pp.132-133 for details.)

COLOURFUL INTERLUDE (*Right*)
A stone urn brimming with luscious, waxy pink busy Lizzies, floss flowers, and tiny silver-leaved plectostachys, forms a pool of colour against a backdrop of evergreen box and honeysuckle. (See p.100 for details.)

COBBLED PATH (*Below*)
Throughout summer, the delicate purple-blue flowers of streptocarpus sit between pots of pelargoniums on a cobbled path. Daisy-like marguerite and felicia flowers, plectostachys, and shrubby solanum sit directly behind.

FROTHY PINKS AND LILACS

☀ SEMI-SHADE   🛠 MEDIUM-RICH POTTING MIX   ⚜ MOIST CONDITIONS

A LOW URN overflowing with floss flowers, busy Lizzies, and silver-leaved plectostachys makes an impressive display. The spectrum of flower colour is limited to a soft palette of lilac-pink, pale pink, and rich pink, framed by a froth of silver-grey foliage. To give of their best, floss flowers need to be kept very moist. Luckily, busy Lizzies enjoy growing in similar conditions and, although plectostachys prefers dry soil, it still performs well in this arrangement. Stand the stone urn on a path where it can be admired from several viewpoints.

◆ GROWING TIPS ◆

Plant up the urn after the chance of frost has passed as busy Lizzies, floss flowers, and plectostachys are all frost tender. Good drainage is important because although floss flowers and busy Lizzies like moist soil, they dislike being waterlogged.

PLECTOSTACHYS
Plectostachys serphyllifolia is a tender evergreen with trails of tiny silver leaves. It makes an attractive alternative to helichrysum; three plants. ●

BUSY LIZZIE
Impatiens New Guinea hybrid in a blend of pale and cyclamen- ● *pink;* three plants.

FLOSS FLOWER
Ageratum houstonianum 'Bengali' originates from Mexico and bears clusters of long-lasting, lilac-pink ● *flowers;* three plants.

Weathered stone urn; ●
40cm (16in) high, 60cm (24in) wide.

Height
65cm
(26in)

HOT COMBINATION

☀ SUN   🌱 RICH POTTING MIX   🖐 MOIST CONDITIONS

LANTANA, WITH ITS SMALL, clustered flowers in a number of hot colour mixes such as pink and yellow, orange and pink, or scarlet and orange, makes a fantastically vibrant container planting. It grows prolifically, so much so that in many tropical countries it is regarded as a weed. Lantana is a poisonous plant, though not deadly, and the aromatic dark green leaves have a strange odour when rubbed between the fingers. Stand a pair of urns brimming with lantana, ornamental coleus foliage, and trailing ivy on either side of a path to create a formal entrance.

◆ GROWING TIPS ◆

Plant up the urns after the last frost as both lantana and coleus are frost tender. Keep both plants bushy by pinching out straggly growth, and remove the coleus' flower spikes.

Height
1m
(3ft)

COLEUS
Coleus blumei. This sun-loving plant from Java produces brick-red leaves with yellow edges; two plants. ●

LANTANA
Lantana camara x hybrida bears flowers that often darken with age so that you see two or more colours ● *in one flowerhead;* four plants.

IVY ●
Hedera helix 'Glacier' has trails of variegated silver leaves that are frost hardy; four plants.

● *Spiral-grooved, reconstituted stone urn; 60cm (24in) deep, 40cm (16in) wide.*

BOLD BLOCKS OF COLOUR

☼ SUN/BRIGHT SHADE 🖌 MEDIUM-RICH POTTING MIX 🪣 MOIST CONDITIONS

W E THINK OF BUSY LIZZIES as shade-loving plants and pelargoniums as sun-lovers; however, they can coexist quite happily in a variety of conditions. The smaller of these two square terracotta pots is planted up with both scarlet and pink pelargoniums. The larger pot has the same type of rich salmon-pink pelargonium, 'Playboy Speckles', and a scarlet-red busy Lizzie with distinctive striped bronze leaves. Place the terracotta pots as a pair on the edge of a path where their startling caps of colour can be viewed to full advantage. Avoid very deep shade or hot, exposed sites, which neither busy Lizzies nor pelargoniums enjoy.

PELARGONIUM ●
Pelargonium 'Friesdorf'
has dark leaves and vivid
scarlet flowers; three plants.

◆ GROWING TIPS ◆

Plant up the pots in spring when all chance of frost has passed. A weekly feed of liquid tomato fertilizer will give you a mass of flowers for several months on end. Remember to dead-head both pelargoniums regularly, and remove any dying busy Lizzie flowers that drop into the pots as they can cause rot. Watch out for aphid infestation early in the season.

Height
80cm
(32in)

Small terracotta cube ●
25cm (10in) deep,
25cm (10in) wide.

In a dry, sunny site, this
display will put on a reliable
show of flamboyant colour
● for four to five months.

PELARGONIUM
Pelargonium 'Playboy Speckles'
boasts pink flowers with random
splashes of darker colour;
● three plants.

BUSY LIZZIE ●
Impatiens New
Guinea hybrid.
A popular choice with
variegated leaves and
brilliant red flowers;
three plants.

● Large terracotta cube
38cm (15in) deep,
38cm (15in) wide.

Paint the terracotta pot ●
with yoghurt to encourage
moss and lichens to grow
on the surface. (See p.10
for details.)

SUGGESTIONS FOR STEPS

RUSTIC JARS (*Left*)
*In summer, a pair of salt-glazed stone jars
planted with dainty purple swan river
daisies and climbing akebia foliage looks
at home on a shallow flight of steps. Bright
yellow alchemilla, growing freely between the
cracks, adds a welcome touch of informality.*

MEDITERRANEAN FLAVOUR (*Right*)
*At the height of summer, steps leading up to
an entrance are brought to life with a row of
terracotta troughs spilling over with hot
pink ivy-leaved pelargonium flowers.*

SHIMMERING PAIR (*Below Left*))
*Add light to dark recesses with bowls of pale
pink petunias, shimmering senecio foliage, and
snapdragons. (See pp.106-107 for details.)*

SCARLET SENTINEL (*Below Right*)
*A wonderful scarlet azalea stands guard at
the foot of a flight of brick steps, producing
a dazzling colour note in late spring.*

DELICATE PINKS

☼ SUN/SEMI-SHADE 🌱 MEDIUM-RICH POTTING MIX 🜲 MOIST CONDITIONS

TWO FLUTED TERRACOTTA BOWLS brimming with pink and silver plants make a very attractive pairing. Pale pink petunias and regal pelargoniums grow among silver foliage, and I've added red snapdragons to create a vibrant colour note. Place the bowls on a flight of entrance steps to give a welcoming touch. Make sure the plantings look attractive from above as well as from the sides, and that the steps are wide enough to take the bowls comfortably and leave plenty of room to walk between them. On narrower steps, a display of several small pots planted up with colourful summer annuals always works well.

Regal pelargoniums and petunia petals are easily damaged in wet and windy weather so place the bowls in a sheltered site. ●

Fluted terracotta bowl, 20cm (8in) deep, ● 40cm (16in) wide.

PETUNIA ●
Petunia 'Apple Blossom'. An attractive pale pink form of one of the most reliable annuals, three plants per bowl.

◆ GROWING TIPS ◆
Plant up these low bowls a little later
than most summer annual plantings
to protect tender regal pelargoniums
from frosts. Deadhead the petunias,
zonal pelargoniums, and snapdragons
regularly and cut back leggy petunia
stems. Take cuttings from the regal
pelargoniums in late summer and
keep in a frost-free place. Plant out
the pelargoniums the following year.

SENECIO
*Senecio maritima 'Silver Dust'
is an annual with fine silvery
foliage that grows quickly;*
● three plants per bowl.

REGAL PELARGONIUM
*Pelargonium 'Lavender Grand Slam'.
A variety with white and pale pink*
● *petals;* two plants per bowl.

● SNAPDRAGON
*Antirrhinum majus 'Floral Showers'
bears fragrant red flowers and grows
exceedingly well in containers;* three
plants per bowl.

● *Fluted terracotta bowl;
20cm (8in) deep,
58cm (23in) wide.*

Height
58cm
(23in)

COOL DUO

☀ SUN/SEMI-SHADE 🗍 MEDIUM-RICH POTTING MIX ⬥ DRY CONDITIONS

A LOW TERRACOTTA BOWL planted with white-flowered, silver-leaved prairie gentian (*Eustoma grandiflorum*) and echeveria – a succulent with silver rosettes of fleshy leaves – presents a cool, elegant display. Prairie gentians have gained in popularity since the introduction of white, cream, purple, and pink varieties, and the hybridization of smaller, carnation-like flowers. A sheltered position on a sunny patio is a suitable site for this planting, as heavy rain can damage the fragile flower petals.

◆ GROWING TIPS ◆

Echeveria is frost tender so plant up the bowl after the chance of frost has passed. Prairie gentian and echeveria prefer almost dry soil. For the best results, feed the display at least once a fortnight with a high potash liquid fertilizer. Bring the planting indoors over the winter months.

PRAIRIE GENTIAN
Eustoma grandiflorum 'Purple picotee' has white poppy-like blooms that flower throughout the summer; four plants.

ECHEVERIA
Echeveria gibbiflora bears fleshy leaves that store water as insurance against drought; three plants.

Low terracotta bowl; 20cm (8in) deep, 60cm (24in) wide.

Height 60cm (24in)

Take care when handling echeveria plants: the waxy leaf bloom easily rubs off.

BLOOD LEAF BOWL

☼ SUN/SEMI-SHADE ⚒ MEDIUM-RICH POTTING MIX ⚱ MOIST CONDITIONS

IN SUMMER CONTAINER PLANTINGS, it need not only be flowers that provide colour. Here, blood leaf offers a vivid contrast of gold and flame-red foliage, which is exaggerated by dividing the bowl into distinct sections. Blood leaf grows to form a mound of brilliant foliage and, for this reason, is often used to produce pattern plantings, such as the floral clocks that were so popular in England in Edwardian garden schemes. Place the container on a patio to add a dash of colour to a dull corner.

◆ GROWING TIPS ◆

Plant up the bowl in early summer in cold areas, after the danger of frost has passed. To encourage healthy leaves, feed the display once every two weeks with a nitrogen fertilizer. Remove flower spikes as they form so that the plant concentrates its energies on producing leaves.

BLOOD LEAF
Iresine lindenii has leaf colour that lasts through the summer until the first frosts; 10 plants.

Remove flowers as they appear to encourage healthy foliage.

Bulbous terracotta bowl; 10cm (4in) deep, 25cm (10in) wide.

Height
43cm
(17in)

MARVEL OF PERU

☀ SUN   ⚒ MEDIUM-RICH POTTING MIX   ⬱ MOIST CONDITIONS

THIS TENDER PERENNIAL is grown from a potato-like tuber, and needs a large pot to give of its best. Marvel of Peru forms a mound of bushy foliage with healthy bright green leaves and a multitude of delicate flower-buds in red, pink, yellow, or white. In this display, there is a mix of carmine-pink and bright yellow blooms; tubers, however, are not sold by colour so the flowers you get are down to chance. Place the pot close to a garden seat so you can see the nocturnal flowers when they are open.

◆ GROWING TIPS ◆
Plant up Marvel of Peru tubers under glass in mid-spring for flowers in mid-summer. When the chance of frost has passed, take the display outside. Feed once a week with a high potash fertilizer and water frequently during the flowering season. Like dahlias, these tubers can be stored through the winter months until spring.

If this species is too large for your pot try 'Pygmea', a more compact plant.

• MARVEL OF PERU
Mirabilis jalapa bears lemon-scented, trumpet-shaped flowers for three months; two tubers.

Flowers open during late afternoon and close the following morning, hence the alternative name,
• *'Four o'clock plant'.*

Height
85cm
(34in)

• *Terracotta pot;
40cm (16in) deep,
20cm (8in) wide.*

SALVIA SPIRES

☼ SUN/SEMI-SHADE ⚒ MEDIUM-RICH POTTING MIX ⬸ MOIST CONDITIONS

VIVID SCARLET SALVIA, *Salvia splendens*, is a half-hardy annual from Brazil, with vibrant, densely-packed flower spikes that last throughout the summer months. On the whole, it requires very little maintenance. In this planting, a mixture of deep pink, coral-pink, and vivid scarlet salvias creates a striking clash of hot colours, which is heightened by the salvias' proximity to silvery plectostachys foliage. This is a rewarding planting for a sunny or semi-shaded paved area.

◆ GROWING TIPS ◆

In cold areas, plant out the salvias in early summer after the likelihood of frost has passed. Encourage bushy growth by pinching out the central flowering tips. Remove dead flower spikes once the bracts turn brown.

PLECTOSTACHYS
Plectostachys serphillifolia needs occasional trimming to keep the trails of foliage in check; three plants.

Rub the silver leaves between the fingertips to release a fresh herby scent.

SALVIA
Salvia splendens 'Phoenix Mixed' *flowers continuously until the first frosts; five plants.*

Weathered terracotta pot; 40cm (16in) deep, 20cm (8in) wide.

Height
80cm
(32in)

AROMATIC APRICOT ROSES

☼ SUN/SEMI-SHADE   ⚒ MEDIUM-RICH POTTING MIX   ⬚ MOIST CONDITIONS

LOW-GROWING ROSES are best suited to container plantings; taller-growing varieties tend not to do so well in confined spaces. This compact shrub, known as 'Sweet Magic Patio', has a continuous display of fragrant, double apricot-orange roses throughout summer and autumn. Planted up with silver-green lotus foliage, the roses appear vivid orange in contrast. The trailing habit of lotus also softens the hard edges of the lead tub. Place the planting next to a garden seat or on a path so you can enjoy the roses' delicious scent.

◆ GROWING TIPS ◆

Plant up the roses in winter or early spring, but introduce lotus at a later stage to avoid hard frosts. Water the roses very occasionally in winter, and more regularly during the flowering season. The roses will grow well for several years in a container this size before needing to be repotted.

ROSE
Rosa 'Sweet Magic Patio'
must be deadheaded regularly to keep the display looking its best through four months of continuous ◆ *flowering;* three plants.

LOTUS
Lotus berthelotii, with its trailing foliage, also grows well in hanging baskets; ◆ four plants.

Antique lead tub; 40cm (16in) deep, ◆ *30cm (12in) wide.*

In late summer, ◆ *lotus foliage carries clusters of scarlet flowers.*

Height
1m
(3ft)

PINK PHLOX WALL BASKET

❄ SEMI-SHADE   🌱 MEDIUM-RICH POTTING MIX   💧 MOIST CONDITIONS

A STRETCH OF BLANK WALL on the side of the house or outbuilding in the garden can be brought to life with one or several basket plantings. This clever use of walls brings flowers and foliage to every area of the garden and is particularly useful when space is at a premium. Here, double pink phlox mixes with trailing helichrysum, plectranthus, and silver vine to produce a reliable, long-lasting display. Make sure that you can reach wall baskets to water them regularly, because they dry out quickly.

◆ GROWING TIPS ◆

Plant up a selection of wall baskets in early summer. Water regularly and feed weekly with a high nitrogen content fertilizer to promote healthy foliage. Deadhead the phlox plants so that they continue to grow strong flowering stems. In autumn, replant silver vine into single pots and bring them indoors as houseplants.

PLECTRANTHUS
Plectranthus coleoides
'Variegatus' flourishes
in the confines of a wall
basket; three plants. ●

PHLOX
Phlox paniculata 'Cherry Pink' is
easily grown, and flowers profusely
● *in late summer; two plants.*

HELICHRYSUM
Helichrysum petiolare
'Variegatum' is a consistent
favourite with container
● *gardeners; one plant.*

Terracotta wall basket; ●
33cm (13in) deep,
45cm (18in) wide.

Height
55cm
(22in)

● SILVER VINE
Scindapsus pictus
'Argyraeus' can
be trained to climb up
a wall; two plants.

MAGNIFICENT LILIES

☀ SUN/SEMI-SHADE 🪴 RICH POTTING MIX 🍴 MOIST CONDITIONS

THE BEAUTY OF MANY LILIES is their trumpet-shaped flowers, and sweet, spicy scent, which cannot be surpassed. Most types of lilies flower in mid-summer; however, it is possible to have lilies in bloom for six months of the year as some flower in early summer and others not until autumn. Place several pots of scented lilies close to the patio where you sit outside, or under an open window so that their perfume wafts into the house on summer evenings.

◆ GROWING TIPS ◆

Plant up the lily bulbs in autumn or spring, depending on availability. As the bulbs grow, feed weekly. In winter protect the plants from frosts. Repot every second year, taking care not to damage the roots.

LILY •
Lilium 'Troubador' is a mid-summer flowering hybrid, derived from such species as L. auratum and L. speciosum; 10 bulbs.

Stake lily stems as soon as the bulbs have been planted, to avoid root damage. •

Painted wooden tub; 33cm (13in) deep, 25cm (10in) wide. •

LILY •
Lilium 'Concorde' is a hybrid derived from such species as L. lancifolium and L. maculatum; 10 bulbs.

Cut off dead flowers. Leave foliage stems, as they are needed to make food for the following year's growth. •

Height
1.2m
(4ft)

LEAFY SELECTION

☀ SHADE/SEMI-SHADE 🖌 MEDIUM-RICH POTTING MIX 🥄 MOIST CONDITIONS

A GLAZED STONEWARE TROUGH brimming with the golden leaves of houttuynia, lysimachia, and pink and burgundy begonias is a particularly lively combination that works well as all the plants enjoy the same growing conditions. Variegated houttuynia thrives within the confines of a container, whereas in garden borders it is more difficult to use because it spreads rapidly and its leaf colour seems at odds with the more subdued tones of other shade-loving plants. Position the trough against a wall in dappled shade. It can remain in this location throughout the summer months until the first frosts.

◆ GROWING TIPS ◆

Plant up the trough in early summer ensuring that there is good drainage. All the plants enjoy copious amounts of water; to encourage healthy, bushy foliage, feed fortnightly with a high nitrogen content plant food.

Height
48cm
(19in)

LYSIMACHIA
Lysimachia nummularia
'Aurea' has leaves that
turn bright greenish-yellow
● *in deep shade; two plants.*

BEGONIA
Begonia semperflorens 'Flamingo' carries
a succession of pink-edged white flowers
for up to four months; two plants.

HOUTTUYNIA
Houttuynia cordata
'Heart of Gold'
bears foliage with a
distinctly tangy aroma;
● *three plants.*

Glazed stoneware trough;
20cm (8in) deep,
● *60cm (24in) long.*

AUTUMN

Clusters of fiery red and orange berries hanging on branches of pyracanthas, cotoneaster, and viburnum shrubs provide container gardeners with a rich palette of autumnal colour. The sun, although low in the sky, still makes its presence felt and brings on the last show of fuchsia, chrysanthemum, and gentian flowers. There is still time to enjoy the pleasure of being outside, to light bonfires, and plant spring bulbs, trees, and shrubs in pots for the year to come. And time also to cherish the warmth of your autumn displays in the glowing midday light.

❧❧

BERRY DISPLAY
Terracotta pots of pyracanthas, low-spreading cotoneaster, and a mopheaded elaeagnus stand against a sun-warmed wall in the golden autumn light. (See p.126 for details.)

FUCHSIA PLANTER

☀ SHADE/SEMI-SHADE ⚒ MEDIUM-RICH POTTING MIX ✇ MOIST CONDITIONS

THERE ARE MANY varieties of fuchsia but they grow in a limited range of colours, from bluey pinks, shades of purple and red, to whites. On the whole, they are graceful shrubs and have an upright, bushy habit. Fuchsias are useful plants to remember when planning container colour because they flower later than most summer annuals, and produce a second wave of blooms in autumn. A paved area at the top of a flight of steps makes a fine setting in which to admire their attractive pendulous flowers.

◆ GROWING TIPS ◆
Plant up tender fuchsia shrubs after the chance of frost has passed. Pinch out a few of the growing tips so that the plants become bushier; at first there are fewer flowers, but in the long term this pays dividends. Most fuchsias cannot tolerate extreme conditions of any kind, whether intense sun or freezing temperatures.

FUCHSIA
Fuchsia 'Cheviot Princess' *is a robust floriferous variety;* four plants. ●

IVY
Hedera helix 'Eva', *with its silvery green and cream leaves, trails around the edge of the container;* four plants. ●

Square plastic Versailles planter; 38cm (15in) *deep,* 38cm (15in) *wide.*

Height 75cm (30in)

LEAFY TROUGH FOR SHADE

❀ SUN/SEMI-SHADE 🛠 MEDIUM-RICH POTTING MIX ⚒ MOIST CONDITIONS

BOLD RED FLOWERS and dark green leaves make a truly vibrant contribution to this decorative terracotta trough, which by early autumn should be brimming with flowers and foliage. The juxtaposition of red and green makes both colours appear even brighter, and in a shady site the busy Lizzies and clusters of begonia flowers really sing out. Position the planting along the edge of a patio wall, to introduce a colourful focal point.

◆ GROWING TIPS ◆

Plant up this trough in summer for autumn flowers. Pinch out the long flowering spires from the coleus plants to promote bushy foliage growth. Repot begonias before the first frosts, and overwinter inside.

Height
70cm
(28in)

BEGONIA
Begonia fuchsioides bears
fuchsia-like flowers in
autumn and winter;
three plants. ◆

BUSY LIZZIE
Impatiens Rosette
Series *can grow to a*
height of 60cm (24in);
three plants. ◆

SPIDER PLANT
Chlorophytum comosum
'Variegatum',
with its evergreen
foliage, provides
year-round interest;
two plants. ◆

COLEUS
Coleus blumei is a type
of coleus with serrated
gold-edged leaves;
two plants. ◆

Pineapple-swagged
terracotta trough;
18cm (7in) deep,
59cm (23in) long. ◆

STARRY MARGUERITES

☀ SUN/SEMI-SHADE 🌡 MEDIUM-RICH POTTING MIX ☄ MOIST CONDITIONS

ARGYRANTHEMUM 'PINK AUSTRALIAN', with its pink double flowers, is a hybrid marguerite which, until recently, had been classified as a member of the chrysanthemum family. Argyranthemums are barely hardy, but they are invaluable for container gardeners as they grow very quickly and produce an abundance of flowers throughout the summer and autumn months. Display this arrangement on a sunny but sheltered terrace to enjoy the daisy-like flowers for months on end.

◆ GROWING TIPS ◆

Plant out after all chance of frost has passed, and remove leggy growths early on so that the plants grow into a sturdy mound. Deadhead the arrangement regularly to encourage the optimum number of flowers. Overwinter agyranthemums, or take cuttings to plant the following year.

Fresh green leaves are characteristic of this perennial.

Height 85cm (34in)

Terracotta pot; 30cm (12in) deep, 20cm (8in) wide.

MARGUERITE
Argyranthemum frutescens 'Pink Australian' has starburst petals with a darker cushion-like central boss; three plants.

MICHAELMAS GLOW

☀ SUN/SEMI-SHADE 🔱 MEDIUM-RICH POTTING MIX ⬸ MOIST CONDITIONS

TWO VARIETIES OF HEUCHERAS, both with dark evergreen leaves, form the core of this inspirational autumn planting: *Heuchera* 'Palace Purple' has plum-coloured leaves and *Heuchera* 'Pewter Moon' has smaller, pewter-coloured leaves with maroon undersides. Here, delicate pink Michaelmas daisies are planted among the heuchera foliage and, by contrast, heighten its depth of colour. Place this display on a paved patio area where it can be viewed from above for maximum impact.

◆ GROWING TIPS ◆

Plant up the display in autumn or spring in a wire vegetable basket lined with moss and plastic to retain moisture. Cut several holes in the plastic lining to allow for drainage. Feed every two weeks with a high potash fertilizer to encourage the Michaelmas daisies to produce a good crop of flowers.

MICHAELMAS DAISY
Aster novi-belgii is fully hardy but often requires treatment against mildew; three plants. ●

HEUCHERA
Heuchera 'Palace Purple', *with its large purple leaves, provides year-round colour;* ● two plants.

HEUCHERA ●
Heuchera 'Pewter Moon' *produces sprays of small white flowers in summer;* two plants.

● *Wire basket lined with moss and plastic;* 20cm (8in) *deep,* 60cm (24in) *wide.*

Height 45cm (18in)

WAYS WITH WALLS

MEDITERRANEAN MIX (*Left*)
A selection of pots containing variegated yuccas and double red nasturtiums, plus bowls of succulents and busy Lizzies, helps to disguise an uninspiring area of wall by adding colour and texture.

TUB OF TULIPS (*Above*)
An almost theatrical statement can be made in the smallest of outdoor spaces by standing a large terracotta pot packed with tulips in front of a salmon-pink wall. 'De Wet' tulips, with their magnificent coloured flowers and delicious scent reminiscent of oranges, are excellent for this container planting. (See p.51 for details.)

AUTUMN COLOUR (*Left*)
In autumn, a copper pot spilling over with osteospermum flowers and the rust-coloured leaves of coleus captures the essence of the season. Here, both the copper container and the planting seem to complement the natural rustic red colour of an old brick garden wall. (See p.127 for details.)

GENTIAN BLUE (*Right*)
The intense blue hue of autumn-flowering gentians, together with the pure white petals of cyclamen, creates a dramatic highlight in an oval-shaped terracotta trough, sitting on an ivy-clad wall. (See p.125 for details.)

HEATHER HARMONY

☼ SUN/SEMI-SHADE   🍴 ACID POTTING MIX   🥄 MOIST CONDITIONS

IN LATE SUMMER AND AUTUMN, caryopteris, the splendid shrub with silvery aromatic leaves, produces tufts of misty blue-lilac flowers. In this display, caryopteris is combined to harmonious effect with an autumn-flowering pale pink heather, whose upright plumes of feathery leaves contrast with trails of variegated green and cream ivy. The square, weather-resistant ceramic container is glazed in glowing deep red – a truly autumnal colour – and looks fantastic situated on a terrace.

◆ GROWING TIPS ◆

Plant up the container in mid-spring. Heather prefers an acid potting mix whereas caryopteris and ivy grow well in any soil. Ensure the potting mix is kept moist; heathers do not enjoy dry growing conditions.

HEATHER
Calluna vulgaris
'Highland Spring'
has clear pink flowers
for up to two months;
● *four plants.*

CARYOPTERIS
Caryopteris x clandonensis
'Heavenly Blue'
flowers prolifically from
late summer to autumn;
two plants. ●——

IVY
Hedera helix
'Sagittifolia
Variegata';
five plants. ●

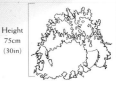

Height
75cm
(30in)

● *Glazed planter;*
28cm (11in) deep,
28cm (11in) wide.

AUTUMN GEMS

☀ SEMI-SHADE   🌿 LIME-FREE POTTING MIX   🧺 MOIST CONDITIONS

THE PURE BLUE COLOUR of gentian flowers is one of the most intense pigments in the plant world. Although gentians are not the easiest plants to cultivate, containerized varieties have a better chance as you can control their growing conditions more closely. Autumn-flowering cyclamen, with its butterfly-like wing petals, enjoys a similar environment, so together they make an extremely happy pair. As an added bonus, this cyclamen has a deliciously sweet perfume. Make the most of the vivid blue of gentians by planting up the display in a warm-coloured terracotta pot, and place it in a sheltered site against a brick wall.

◆ GROWING TIPS ◆

Plant up the container in summer in lime-free potting mix. Gentian and cyclamen are frost hardy but need a sheltered site, especially during cold winters. Every two or three years, remember to divide and repot all the plants during the spring months.

Height
30cm
(12in)

CYCLAMEN
Cyclamen cyprium, a tuberous-rooted plant, produces fragrant blooms from early autumn to • *spring; three plants.*

Cyclamen is found growing wild in woods and mountainous areas in • *Mediterranean countries.*

GENTIAN
Gentiana sino-ornata 'Inverleith', like other Asiatic gentians, flowers in autumn, whereas European species flower throughout spring; two plants. •

Ensure the •
soil is lime-free or the leaves of this species will turn yellow.

• *Oval-shaped terracotta trough; 16cm (6in) deep, 35cm (14in) long.*

FIERY PYRACANTHAS

✺ SUN/SEMI-SHADE   ⚒ MEDIUM-RICH POTTING MIX   ⚏ MOIST CONDITIONS

Pyracanthas are very handsome, strong-growing plants with needle-like thorns. For this reason, they are often grown as boundary hedges. Among their many attributes are their evergreen leaves, white clusters of hawthorn-like flowers, and long-lasting red, orange, or yellow berries. In open ground, most pyracanthas grow into large shrubs or small trees, but they also do very well in pots, and can be trained by growing them on a trellis or cane pyramid. A sheltered site against a wall or fence is an ideal location for these attractive shrubs.

PYRACANTHA
Pyracantha rogersiana
'Golden Charmer'
bears spires of white
flowers in summer,
which give way to
vibrant orange-
yellow berries;
one shrub. ◆

PYRACANTHA ◆
Pyracantha rogersiana
'Orange Charmer' *has*
small evergreen leaves and
glossy red-orange berries in
autumn; one shrub.

Support the shrub as it ◆
grows with a cane trellis.
(See p.150 for details.)

◆ GROWING TIPS ◆

Plant up pots between autumn and spring. Tie in shoots as necessary to maintain the shape of the shrubs, and cut back unwanted shoots as they appear. Bear in mind that heavy pruning will reduce the number of summer flowers and autumn berries. Pyracanthas are prone to diseases, such as fireblight and scab, but these two varieties are known for their natural resistance. Water freely in summer and feed every two weeks.

Terracotta pot; ◆
33cm (13in) deep,
20cm (8in) wide.

Height
1.5m
(5ft)

AUTUMN DAISIES

☀ SUN   🖌 MEDIUM-RICH POTTING MIX   🥄 MOIST CONDITIONS

OSTEOSPERMUM IS A MEMBER of the daisy family. This variety has enchanting daisy flowers, with pale pink petals and dark purple eyes, which it produces in huge quantities in summer and autumn. Here, in a copper bowl, the aromatic silver-green leaves of osteospermum, interspersed with rust-coloured coleus foliage, present a wonderful autumnal show. Both plants are perennial, but neither is hardy and so will not survive beyond the first autumn frosts. Place the copper bowl in a sheltered but sunny spot to keep the planting looking its best.

◆ GROWING TIPS ◆

Plant up the pot with osteospermum and coleus in early summer. Feed weekly with a high potash fertilizer to encourage a mass of blooms in autumn. Deadhead osteospermum flowers as they finish, and remove flower spikes and straggly growth from the coleus plants to keep the arrangement looking bushy.

COLEUS
Coleus blumei is also known as flame nettle because of its brick-red, nettle-like leaves; two plants. ●

OSTEOSPERMUM
Osteospermum barberiae is a tender perennial that flowers for up to three ● *months;* four plants.

Height
80cm
(32in)

Weather-beaten copper pot; 15cm (6in) deep, ● 25cm (10in) wide.

CHEERY CHRYSANTHEMUMS

☀ SUN   ⚒ MEDIUM-RICH POTTING MIX   ✇ MOIST CONDITIONS

CHRYSANTHEMUMS have bold rust, maroon, plum, orange, gold, or red flowers and are synonymous with autumn. Young plants can be easily purchased from garden centres, and grown in pots. They are rewarding plants, producing a prolific display of blooms that last over several weeks. Chrysanthemums grow naturally to form a low mound of flowers but they can be trained into pyramids or mopheads. Place several pots of red, orange, and yellow plants as a group on a paved area to bring vivid autumn colour to your patio.

A single plant can produce hundreds of flowers in one season. ●

CHARM ●
CHRYSANTHEMUM
Chrysanthemum 'Zuki' is a dwarf plant that produces a multitude of star-shaped single flowers; one plant.

CHARM CHRYSANTHEMUM ●
Chrysanthemum 'Moonlight' has single daisy-like flowers and a sweet tangy perfume; one plant.

◆ GROWING TIPS ◆

Plant up chrysanthemums in a bright,
sheltered position in early summer.
Feed once a week with a high potash
content solution until the buds begin
to show colour in late summer.
Remove long straggly shoots
to encourage bushy plants.
Water frequently but try
not to saturate the soil.

SPRAY CHRYSANTHEMUM
Chrysanthemum x *hybrida has
long, tubular petals that form a
● spiky outline; three plants.*

● *Long terracotta tom;
40cm (16in) deep,
15cm (6in) wide.*

● *Long terracotta tom;
60cm (24in) deep,
15cm (6in) wide.*

Height
75cm
(30in)

WINTER

In winter, strong simple shapes made by trees and shrubs without leaves become elegant features in town and country gardens. Well-clipped topiary in plain glazed containers enhances this simple austerity, while other varieties of evergreens with pale green, silver, or gold foliage add a subtle beauty to displays. Indoors, the same pale beauty is offered by winter-flowering plants, such as jasmine and narcissus with their rich scents. For a flamboyant display of colour, we need to turn to poinsettias, orchids, and other tropical plants to usher us through the winter months.

❧❧

CHEERY WINDOW BOX
A terracotta trough of hardy evergreens can survive several degrees of frost. Here Leucothoë 'Scarletta' has rich claret-coloured leaves that mix beautifully with the brilliant red and orange berries of winter cherry. (See p.142 for details.)

RED WINTER BERRIES

☀ SEMI-SHADE   ▯ ACID POTTING MIX   ⚲ MOIST CONDITIONS

I'VE ACHIEVED a cheery small-scale planting by growing winter-green, with its fat red berries and glossy leaves, and silvery blue juniper in a copper bowl. Both plants are extremely hardy, which makes them an ideal choice for a winter planting. Wintergreens are often thought to be invasive plants and some, such as *Gaultheria shallon*, use suckers to spread out over large areas. *Gaultheria procumbens*, used in this display, is not as invasive as other species and will mature quite happily for a couple of years within the confines of the container. Likewise, *Juniperus squamata* 'Blue Carpet' does well in containers; in the open it will spread further to form a carpet of foliage up to 2m (6ft) wide. Place the copper bowl on the edge of a path to add interest to winter borders.

JUNIPER •
Juniperus squamata 'Blue Carpet'
spreads out its branches of aromatic
silvery blue foliage; two plants.

◆ GROWING TIPS ◆

Plant up the container in autumn or late spring in cold areas to enable the wintergreens to establish themselves, as young plants can be damaged by frosts. Handle the juniper plants with gloves as they can cause a skin rash. Stand the pot in semi-shade away from trees dripping with rainwater, which wintergreens dislike. During summer, feed the display fortnightly with a high potash content food to encourage a good crop of red winter berries. Trim long juniper shoots to keep the foliage under control.

WINTERGREEN
*Gaultheria procumbens, with its
aromatic glossy green leaves, is
a fast-growing, creeping species
that can spread up to 1m (3ft)
● across; two plants.*

*Leaves and fruit yield
wintergreen oil, which is
● used to flavour toothpaste.*

*● During winter months
aromatic red berries
follow white or pink
summer flowers.*

*● Tarnished copper pot,
22cm (8in) deep,
30cm (12in) wide.*

Height
30cm
(12in)

MINTY EVERGREENS

☀ SUN/SEMI-SHADE　🖌 MEDIUM-RICH POTTING MIX　🥄 MOIST CONDITIONS

I T IS EASY TO ASSUME that all evergreens have dark, sombre green foliage similar to laurel or yew. However, there are many with pale green, silver, or gold foliage that can add a luminous quality to winter arrangements. Here, gold-edged hebe leaves, silvery green-leaved senecio, gold and green euonymus, and cream-and-green-leaved ivy grow in a white window box. All of these shrubs thrive in a container environment. To appreciate this low-maintenance display fully, place it on a window-ledge where it will flourish all through the year.

◆ GROWING TIPS ◆

Plant up the window box in autumn or spring. Keep the arrangement well watered through the summer months; water sparingly during warm winter spells, but not at all in freezing cold weather conditions.

Height
85cm
(34in)

SENECIO
Senecio 'Sunshine' has leaves coated in a silvery felt which are soft to touch; two plants.

EUONYMUS
Euonymus fortunei 'Emerald and Gold' has low-growing evergreen foliage and thrives in containers; one plant.

HEBE
Hebe elliptica 'Variegata' tolerates atmospheric pollution and salty winds; one plant.

IVY
Hedera helix is easy to cultivate as it will grow in any soil or aspect; five plants.

Weatherboard window box; 45cm (18in) deep, 85cm (34in) wide.

CHRISTMAS BASKET

☀ BRIGHT SHADE ⚒ MEDIUM-RICH POTTING MIX ✲ DRY CONDITIONS

D URING WINTER, indoor container plantings come into their own, and this spectacular rustic basket packed with pink-striped cyclamen and stippled gold-leaved pick-a-back plant is no exception. Many indoor-flowering plants, such as cyclamen, find it difficult to survive in centrally-heated rooms at this time of year. To prolong the life of this display over the Christmas period, make sure you buy the cyclamen plants in peak condition and place the basket in a cool, draught-free site on a bright window-ledge.

◆ GROWING TIPS ◆
In autumn, plant up cyclamens in pots for indoor flowering with the top half of their tubers just above soil level. To delay flowering until Christmas, remove the first cyclamen buds. Water the display sparingly at the base of the pick-a-back plant.

● CYCLAMEN
Cyclamen persicum 'Giganteum' has flowers that last longer if a steady temperature of 12ºC (55ºF) is maintained; two plants.

PICK-A-BACK PLANT
Tolmiea menzeisii produces baby plants on top of the larger leaves, weighing them down so that they droop over the sides; ● two plants.

Heart-shaped leaves are blotched with silver. ●

Rustic wicker basket; 16cm (6in) deep, 56cm (22in) wide. ●

Height 45cm (18in)

TRADITIONAL TOPIARY

☼ SUN/BRIGHT SHADE 🖌 MEDIUM-RICH POTTING MIX ⬦ MOIST CONDITIONS

THE GREAT JOY OF TOPIARY is that it looks fantastic throughout the year, but it comes into its own in winter when well-clipped evergreens in simple geometric shapes, such as cones, cubes, pyramids, and domes, give the often bare garden an architectural formality. Box and yew in particular, and shrubs with tight-knit foliage such as bay, can be trained or clipped into almost any form, and require the minimum of maintenance outside the growing season. Plant up topiary trees in frost-proof pots to bring interest to patios through the year.

Sweet bay is one of the few laurels that • *is not poisonous.*

SWEET BAY •
Laurus nobilis grows best in a sheltered site as it is not the hardiest of shrubs; young leaves can be easily damaged by chill winds; one tree.

Aromatic, evergreen • *leaves. Bay plants are traditionally trimmed into mophead shapes.*

◆ GROWING TIPS ◆

Plant up the ceramic pots in autumn or spring. For healthy foliage, feed monthly during the growing season with a nitrogen-rich fertilizer. Before frosts, trim all the topiary trees into shape. In warm winter spells, water the bay tree to keep the potting mix just moist. Box trees need much less frequent watering during mild winter spells. Withhold water altogether from both species when the ground temperature falls below freezing during winter months.

Large glazed pot; 50cm (20in) deep, 75cm (30in) wide.

COMMON BOX

Buxus sempervirens is a quick-growing species. Clip regularly to maintain its shape; one tree per pot. ●

Buxus sempervirens with its densely-packed foliage was a favourite topiary plant in Roman times. ●

Box is hardy enough to remain outside through-out even the most severe winter weather. ●

● Jade-green glazed pot, 38cm (15in) deep, 48cm (19in) wide.

Height
1m
(3ft)

CONTAINERS IN CONSERVATORIES

FRAGRANT FLOWERS (*Left*)
Before the first frosts, bring individual pots of jasmine and narcissus into a warm, light-filled conservatory or garden room. They will produce a succession of flowers throughout the winter months and will fill the room with their sweet buttery scent. (See p.140 for details.)

EXOTIC GARDEN ROOM (*Below*)
Sophisticated-looking plants, such as these cymbidium orchids and crimson azaleas, enjoy the cool but sheltered environment of a bright garden room through the winter. They will both flower prolifically into the following spring, when they can be placed outdoors in their containers.

ARMCHAIR COMPANIONS (*Above*)
Bring summer into a semi-shady area of a conservatory by planting up individual pots of regal pelargoniums and frothy white hydrangea mopheads. Maidenhair ferns also look attractive, forming an umbrella of cool green foliage.

INDOOR HANGING BASKET (*Below*)
A mass of deep pink bell-shaped flowers of Kalanchoë 'Wendy' looks fantastic spilling over the edges of a late-winter hanging basket in a sheltered conservatory room.

FRAGRANT WHITES

☼ BRIGHT SHADE 🔱 MEDIUM-RICH POTTING MIX ⚚ MOIST CONDITIONS

JASMINE AND PAPER WHITE NARCISSUS both carry white flowers with a deliciously sweet fragrance, making them an attractive winter pairing. *Jasminum polyanthum* is a half-hardy climbing species, whose branching stems are bursting with clouds of white star-like flowers by mid-winter. *Narcissus* 'Paper White Grandiflora' produces a succession of flowers from early winter until mid-spring. Both plants are frost tender and need to be grown indoors; their fragrance is so magnificent that no house or conservatory should ever be without them.

◆ GROWING TIPS ◆

In summer and early autumn, plant up jasmine in pots outdoors, and feed fortnightly with a high potash food. Bring indoors before the first autumn frost. During the flowering season, water freely and deadhead regularly. Plant narcissus bulbs in bulb fibre six weeks before you want them to bloom. Keep the soil moist, and store the bulbs in a dark room until shoots appear, and then place them out in a bright but sheltered situation.

• JASMINE
Jasminum polyanthum is thought to flower best when its stems are trained horizontally, so try growing the plant around a wire hoop or over a bamboo trellis; one plant.

• PAPER WHITE NARCISSUS
Narcissus 'Paper White Grandiflora' has about eight flowers to a stem. Stake the stems to keep them upright; 15 bulbs.

Moss-and-plastic-lined wire wastepaper basket; 30cm (12in) deep, • 25cm (10in) wide.

Green metal bucket; 25cm (10in) deep • 27cm (11in) wide.

Height 1m (3ft)

BUDDING SKIMMIAS

☼ SEMI-SHADE ⚱ RICH POTTING MIX 🌢 MOIST CONDITIONS

SKIMMIAS ARE APPEALING SHRUBS for winter plantings as they bear aromatic evergreen leaves and decorative clusters of flower-buds that stay intact until spring. Viburnum also carries flower-buds in winter, though they may burst into flower during spells of mild weather. The final ingredient is gold variegated ivy, whose trailing leaves look sunny all year round. Plant up this mix in a clay urn to make an attractive focal point for a patio or terrace, and position it where it can be seen from a haven of warmth inside.

◆ GROWING TIPS ◆

Plant up the container in autumn or spring. During the growing season, feed monthly with a high potash content fertilizer. This planting can remain in the same container for several years; even when it is not in flower, the foliage will continue to look fresh and attractive for the remainder of the year.

SKIMMIA
Skimmia japonica 'Rubella' may suffer damage to young leaves during severe frost;
• *two plants.*

VIBURNUM •
Viburnum tinus 'Eve Price' produces bright pink buds that open out into pale pink flowers; one plant.

SKIMMIA •
Skimmia laureola has cream flower-buds and, like other skimmias, can tolerate atmospheric pollution; two plants.

IVY
Hedera helix 'Harald' has evergreen leaves with bright gold edges; four plants. •

Height
80cm
(32in)

• *Smooth clay urn; 33cm (13in) deep, 50cm (20in) wide.*

WINTER CHERRIES

☀ SUN/SEMI-SHADE   ⚒ ACID POTTING MIX   ⬧ DRY CONDITIONS

$\mathbf{F}$OR THOSE OF US WHO LIVE in temperate climates, there are a number of attractive plants that can be added to the outdoor palette and, although not hardy, will survive the winter weather if placed in a sheltered site. Winter cherry, with its shiny orange berries, is a colourful choice – as are azaleas. Here, I've planted up winter cherry with the maroon and green leaves of leucothoë, and a swathe of trailing ivy. Place the terracotta trough against a wall or on a window-sill, to shelter it from harsh elements.

◆ GROWING TIPS ◆

Plant up the terracotta trough in autumn. Providing the temperature does not drop below 7°C (45°F), the winter cherry, leucothoë, and ivy will last for two years. Keep the soil almost dry, and withhold water in freezing conditions. Feed fortnightly.

IVY
Hedera helix 'Glacier'
trails down to break up
the horizontal thrust of
the winter display;
• *five plants.*

LEUCOTHOE
Leucothoë fontanesiana 'Scarletta'
carries attractive evergreen foliage
throughout the year;
two plants. •

WINTER CHERRY
Solanum pseudocapsicum has star-
shaped white flowers in summer,
followed by scarlet fruit in winter;
three plants. •

Height
60cm
(24in)

• *Swag-motif*
terracotta trough;
20cm (10in) deep,
45cm (18in) wide.

RUSTIC INDOOR BASKET

☼ BRIGHT SHADE ⚒ MEDIUM-RICH POTTING MIX ⚲ MOIST CONDITIONS

THE WINTER HOLIDAY is a time to bring decorative container plantings indoors. Here, pale pink azaleas are planted up with soft pink-and-cream-coloured poinsettia foliage, and bright scarlet and yellow primulas. All three plants enjoy similar growing conditions and are readily available at garden centres. Place this rustic basket on a bright window-ledge away from radiators; the cooler the room the longer the arrangement will last.

◆ GROWING TIPS ◆

Plant up the basket in late autumn, and remember to cut drainage holes in the plastic lining. Choose plants with plenty of buds that are just coming into flower. The azalea likes to be well watered: do not allow its fibrous roots to dry out.

POINSETTIA
Euphorbia pulcherrima 'Peaches and Cream' produces a poisonous milky white sap, so wash your hands after handling this plant; one plant. ●

AZALEA
Rhododendron 'Pink Pearl' is an evergreen hybrid that carries soft pink flowers until spring; one plant. ●

Azaleas like more water than the other plants in the basket so water the display liberally ● from the right-hand side.

PRIMULA
Primula vulgaris hybrid is suitable for containers, although it is chiefly ● grown outdoors; three plants.

Plastic-lined ● twig basket; 15cm (6in) deep, 35cm (14in) wide.

Height
45cm
(18in)

PLANT CARE

*E*quip yourself with a few basic tools, such as a hand trowel and a watering can, and follow the simple measures outlined on these pages to establish the best growing and flowering conditions for your plants. Techniques for preparing containers and then potting the different types of plant in tubs, window boxes, and hanging baskets are carefully explained. Practical advice is given on how to maintain a long-lasting display, and there is also information on repotting plants, supporting stems, and training shrubs.

❧❦

STARTING FROM SCRATCH
Choose a suitable container from the enormous range now available, purchase your plants, potting mix, and trowel, and you will be ready to try your hand at container gardening.

PREPARING CONTAINERS

With all containers, whether made of terracotta, ceramic, stone, concrete, or wood, it is a good idea to remove any soil from the pots, and scrub out the inside with disinfectant. By following these simple measures you will prevent pests and diseases, which might be present on the container's porous surface, infesting and infecting your healthy plants, and therefore give them the best possible start for a long-lasting display.

CLEAN START
To disinfect porous containers and the broken pieces of clay flowerpot that your are using as crocks, you will need germicide solution, a hard scrubbing brush, and a bucket of clean water with which to rinse out the inside of the container thoroughly.

1 Using a hard brush, scrub out the inside of the container with germicide solution, to kill bacteria and fungal spores.

2 Cover the drainage hole with crocks, concave-side down, to help water find a way of escaping through the bottom.

COMPOST

POTTING MIXES
When planting up containers, buy bags of ready-made neutral, acid, or alkaline potting mix at the garden centre. Add compost to enrich the mix, coconut fibre to improve the texture, and sand and gravel to encourage good drainage.

GRAVEL

SAND

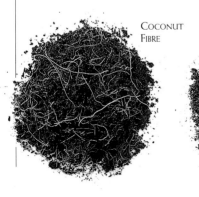

COCONUT
FIBRE

POTTING
MIX

SHRUB PLANTING

Careful planting will determine whether a plant flourishes and is long-lasting, or wilts and has a shortened lifespan. Once you have cleaned out the container, and placed several crocks over the drainage hole, start filling the pot with the appropriate potting mix. If the container is fairly large, it is best to fill it layer by layer, firming gently with your fingertips. This avoids compacting the soil, which would inhibit drainage.

SELECTING PLANTS

Choose plants with compact, healthy foliage and a good strong root system. Avoid plants with sparse stems and densely packed roots.

1 Fill the pot three-quarters full with soil, and press in the plant's original pot to establish how much space the shrub needs.

2 Loosen the tightly packed soil and roots and, holding the shrub firmly at the base of the stem, lower it into the pot.

3 Firm new soil around the sides of the root ball, building up the soil until it reaches the same level as the soil around the shrub.

4 Water the shrub thoroughly after planting. Remember that porous terracotta pots soak up moisture especially quickly.

CONDITIONING PLANTS

Before planting, dip the plant in its plastic pot into a bucket of cold water. Hold the pot just below the water level for a few seconds, until all air bubbles are released from the potting mix, and it is thoroughly moist.

WINDOW BOX PLANTING

Prepare the window box (*see p.146*) and, before you begin planting, place it *in situ*, partly filled with moistened potting mix as it will be too heavy to lift on to a window-ledge when it is packed with plants and watered. Always plant as generously as possible so that flowers and foliage spill over the edges as they grow. Leave space for fast-growing plants to expand, but bring slow-growers close together. When complete, give all the plants a thorough watering and feed them regularly as they grow to keep them healthy. When the flowers are past their best, dig out the plants (*see p.153*) and replace with another selection.

1 Before planting, work out where you want to place each plant and how many you need. I usually place tall plants towards the back of the box, and trailing plants along the front and sides.

2 Lift each plant out of its pot by placing your fingers across the base of the stem and turning the pot upside-down; tap the pot on a hard edge and extract the plant. Gently loosen the roots.

3 Continue planting, working from right to left, firming the soil with your fingertips around each plant as you go. Lastly, fill in the sides of the container with potting mix to just below the rim.

PLANTING UP BULBS

For a striking show of flowers, grow plenty of bulbs in each pot. The planting depth depends on the bulb size. As a general rule, plant each bulb at a depth that equates to twice its own depth.

1 Using your fingertips, set the bulbs firmly in the pot, allowing a little space between each one.

2 Cover the bulbs in potting mix, up to 2.5cm (1in) below the container rim. Firm gently.

LAYERS OF BULBS
To make the most of available space, plant layers of different bulbs in one container. These will then flower at different times during the season. Here I've planted early-flowering crocuses just below the surface, with later-flowering tulips somewhat deeper in the container.

Hanging Basket Planting

I usually overplant hanging baskets because they look most spectacular when overflowing with flowers and have plenty of trailing foliage. A hanging basket has a rounded base so it is a good idea to stand it in a plastic pot when planting to keep it steady and prevent it toppling over. Ensure that the basket sits high on the pot so that plants can be threaded into the sides of the display.

EQUIPMENT
You will need moss, a garden refuse sack, scissors, potting mix, and several plants.

1 Balance the basket on a pot, uncouple the chains, and line the interior with sphagnum moss.

2 Next, insert a plastic lining and pierce with scissors for drainage. Add some potting mix.

3 Prepare the plants you wish to thread through the sides of the basket by wrapping in plastic.

4 Using scissors, make about seven long slits in the basket's plastic lining. Working from the inside to the outside, thread through each wrapped plant.

5 Slide the plastic off each plant, and gently pack moist potting mix around the roots. Begin filling out the main body of the display with flowering plants.

6 Place larger plants towards the middle and trailing plants at the sides, building up the level of potting mix as you go. Hang the basket *in situ* before watering.

STAKING AND TRAINING

Staking is one of the best ways to provide support for the flexible stems of free-standing plants in containers, especially those situated in exposed sites. Tall perennials and annuals require only single stakes, while climbers, shrubs, and trees may need a sturdier tripod of canes or a trellis. Some trees and shrubs can be trained to create a variety of interesting plant shapes.

● Check how high the shrub is likely to grow, to ensure that the stakes are long enough from the outset.

Tie the top ● of the trellis to a wall to keep it steady.

Choose a ● heavy, frost-proof terracotta or stone pot; shallow pots are not suitable for staked plants.

● Bury the legs of the trellis in the potting mix before planting to avoid damaging the shrub's roots.

DISCIPLINED PYRACANTHAS
Here, two pyracantha shrubs are staked in different ways: one is trained on a bamboo trellis to grow flush against a wall; the other is supported by a wigwam of bamboo stakes and is free-standing.

CONSTRUCTING A BAMBOO TRELLIS

To make a gently widening trellis, you will need four 1.5m- (5ft-) long garden canes and nine 35cm- (14in-) long canes, garden wire, a pair of pliers, and secateurs. Lay the shorter garden canes across the longer ones, and tie them together with garden wire as described below.

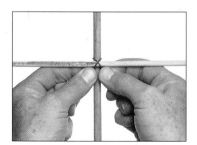

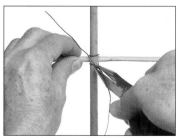

1 Position one vertical and one horizontal piece of bamboo cane at right angles and bind them togther around the join in an X-shape with garden wire.

2 Use a pair of pliers to tighten the binding on the reverse side. Attach the bottom and top rung first, and then evenly space the other canes between the two.

TRELLIS SUPPORT
Ensure that the four legs of the bamboo trellis fit comfortably into the width of the pot before you start to bind the trellis canes together with garden wire or string.

TRAINING A STANDARD FUCHSIA

1 At a height of about 15cm (6in), remove all sideshoots to encourage rapid upward growth.

2 As the plant grows, continue to remove sideshoots, and tie the mast stem to a bamboo cane.

3 At 1m (3ft) tall, allow three more sets of leaves to form, and pinch out the growing tip.

4 At 15cm (6in) long, pinch out the tips of the sideshoots so that they will branch once more.

STANDARD FUCHSIA
Feed with a nitrogen-rich fertilizer twice weekly until the stem has grown, then use a potash-rich fertilizer three times a week.

CLIPPING AND SHAPING TOPIARY TREES

1 Using secateurs, carefully trim the young box plant into a cone shape, making sure that you do not cut the main growing tip.

2 At a height of 1m (3ft), use shears to trim the tree into a cone shape. Lean a cane against the sides to act as a cutting guide.

3 Maintain the shape of the mature box by trimming the tree at least twice a year, during the spring and summer months.

PLANT MAINTENANCE

Plants grown in containers are quite simple to look after if you water, feed, and deadhead them as recommended in the *Growing Tips* that accompany all the planting projects. As a general rule, use high potash content liquid plant food during the growing season to produce the maximum number of flowers, and high nitrogen content fertilizers to ensure healthy and bushy foliage growth.

DEADHEADING

Cut off dead blooms at the stem joint to prolong the flowering season; leave them on the plant if you want berries or seedheads.

TOP-DRESSING

1 Most shrubs can grow in the same pot for a few years if they are nourished with compost. First, scrape off about 5cm (2in) of soil.

2 Using a trowel, replace this top layer of soil with some fresh compost mixed with a slow-release fertilizer, then water well.

REPOTTING SPRING BULBS

Bulbs, especially narcissi, do not like to be overcrowded. It is best to repot them each year, in autumn; otherwise they will not flower well and will produce undersized or unhealthy foliage. When you are repotting, remove any rotting or dead bulb material to maintain a healthy planting.

1 Turn out the contents of the pot and carefully pick out the bulbs, discarding any damaged ones.

2 Separate out clumps of bulbs by gently pulling them apart, and remove loose outer layers.

REPLANTED BULBS
Dust the bulbs with a fungicidal powder and plant in moist potting mix (see p.148).

REPLANTING

By the end of summer, the flowering annuals in hanging baskets are often past their best, though foliage plants, such as ivy, remain healthy and can be retained in the display as the foundation for the next season's planting.

REPLANTING A HANGING BASKET

1 Using a hand trowel, carefully dig out all the spent summer-flowering annuals. Loosen the soil and fill in with fresh if necessary.

2 Plant a selection of evergreens or winter-flowering plants in their place. Firm the soil and then water the basket thoroughly.

REJUVENATED PLANTING
Hardy plants, such as skimmias and heathers, will thrive in winter if they are planted in an acid-based potting mix.

REPOTTING A TIRED-LOOKING SHRUB

1 Repot a shrub if its leaves are wilting and if it lacks vigour. First, ease out the shrub from its pot and loosen the root ball.

2 Place several clean crocks and potting mix in the base of the new pot, which should be about 5cm (2in) wider than the old one.

3 Centre the plant and fill in with potting mix, firming as you go until the soil level is the same as in the previous pot.

PLANT LIST

TREES AND SHRUBS

Abutilon x hybridum
(Abutilon)
Frost-tender, evergreen shrub.
Varieties carry red, pink, and
yellow bell-shaped, pendent
flowers throughout summer and
autumn months. Plant in sun in
well-drained, medium-rich potting
mix, and keep well watered.

Argyranthemum
(Marguerite)
Frost-tender, evergreen shrub.
Several species produced many
cultivars with profusion of single
and double daisy flowers in red,
pink, yellow, and white in summer
and autumn. Grow in sun in well-
drained, medium-rich potting mix,
and feed weekly in summer.

Artemisia 'Silver Brocade'
(Artemisia)
Frost-hardy, evergreen, spreading
sub-shrub with silvery aromatic
leaves and yellow flowers in
summer. Plant in sunny site in
medium-rich potting mix.

Buxus sempervirens
(Common Box)
Frost-hardy, evergreen shrub or
tree. Grow in sun or bright shade
in medium-rich potting mix. Feed
monthly in growing season.

Calluna vulgaris
(Heather)
Frost-hardy, evergreen shrub.
Grow in sun or semi-shade in
acid potting mix. Feed weekly in
summer and autumn months, and
water well with rainwater.

Camellia japonica
(Camellia)
Evergreen shrub producing single
and double flowers in red, pink,
cream, and white in spring.
Protect from early morning sun
and grow in semi-shade in well-
drained, acid potting mix.

Caryopteris clandonensis
(Caryopteris)
Medium-sized deciduous shrub
with aromatic silver leaves and
whorls of feathery blue flowers in
late summer and autumn. Grow in
sun or semi-shade in well-drained,
medium-rich potting mix.

Euonymus fortunei
(Euonymus)
Evergreen shrub with attractive
leaves. Well-suited to pot culture.
Plant in medium-rich potting mix
in sun or semi-shade. Water well
in growing season.

Euphorbia pulcherrima
(Poinsettia)
Part of large genus of both
temperate and tropical shrubs.
Often grown as indoor plant for
Christmas market. Keep out of
draughts and ensure that potting
mix is kept moist.

Fuchsia
Frost-tender, evergreen shrubs
that are deciduous in cooler
temperatures. Large number of
flowering varieties available. Late
summer and autumn are best
flowering seasons. Grow in well-
drained, medium-rich or rich
potting mix, in semi-shaded site.
Feed well during growing season
and water regularly.

Gaultheria procumbens
(Wintergreen)
Evergreen, spreading sub-shrub
with small, glossy green leaves
turning red in winter. White
flowers followed by scarlet berries
in autumn and winter. Grow in
shade or semi-shade in well-
drained, acid potting mix. Keep
plants well watered throughout
growing season.

Hebe
Large genus of evergreen shrubs
with racemes of flowers in pinks,
purples, and whites. Variegated-
leaved hebes, such as *H. elliptica*,
are useful for winter container
plantings in sheltered sites. Plant
in sun or semi-shade in well-
drained, medium-rich potting mix.

Hedera
(Ivy)
Evergreen climbers and trailers
that are ideal for pot culture, both
as secondary and main features in
plantings. Leaves vary from rich
green through gold, silver, and
cream variegations. Grow in any
exposure in well-drained, medium-
rich, preferably alkaline, potting
mix. Keep well watered through
growing season.

Helichrysum petiolare
(Helichrysum)
Trailing, evergreen shrub grown
as annual for its foliage. Varieties
have silver, gold, and variegated
leaves. Grow in any well-drained
potting mix. *Helichrysum petiolare* is
excellent for hanging baskets or
plant to trail over edges in troughs,
sinks, tubs, and pots.

Hydrangea macrophylla
(Hydrangea)
Deciduous shrub with mopheaded
flowers in red, pink, white, and
blue. Grow in semi-shade in acid
potting mix, and water well in
growing season.

Jasminum polyanthum
(Jasmine)
Frost-tender, evergreen climber
producing fragrant white flowers
in winter. Grow indoors in cool
garden room or conservatory in
medium-rich potting mix. Keep
well watered, and feed fortnightly
with high potash food.

Juniperus squamata
(Juniper)
Evergreen, spreading conifer with
intense silvery blue leaves. Grow
in sun or semi-shade in well-
drained, medium-rich potting
mix. Water sparingly.

Lantana camara
(Lantana)
Frost-tender, evergreen shrub
with a long succession of flowers.
Cultivars are available in hot pink,
red, orange, yellow, and white.
Grow in sun in rich potting mix.

Laurus nobilis
(Bay)
Evergreen tree with aromatic
leaves, usually grown in container
as clipped shrub. Grow in sun or
semi-shade in well-drained, rich
potting mix. Keep just moist and
water throughout winter months,
except when temperature falls
below freezing.

Leucothöe fontanesiana
(Leucothöe)
Evergreen shrub with white bell-
shaped flowers in spring. Several
varieties have colourful leaves.
Grow in well-drained, acid
potting mix, in sheltered site
in shade or semi-shade.

Plectostachys serphyllifolia
(Plectostachys)
Frost-tender, evergreen shrub
with small trailing silvery leaves.
Grow in well-drained, medium-
rich potting mix in sunny or semi-
shaded position. Plectostachys
looks attractive in hanging baskets
and trailing over edges of pots.

Prunus
(Cherry)
Deciduous trees with double pink
blossoms in spring. Cut back
stems after flowering to encourage
new flowers for following season.
Plant in well-drained, medium-
rich potting mix in sunny sites.

Pyracantha rogersiana
(Pyracanthas)
Evergreen shrub with white
flowers in summer followed by
red, orange, and yellow berries.
Plant in sun or semi-shade in well-
drained, medium-rich potting mix.
Keep well watered in summer. If
necessary, support this tall-
growing shrub with stakes.

Rhododendron
(Rhododendron, Azalea)
Evergreen and deciduous shrubs
and trees with showy flowers in
all colours but true blue. Grow all
species in acid potting mix in
semi-shade, sheltered from cold
winds. Azaleas are generally
small-leaved and dwarf shrubs
with profuse blooms.

Rosa
(Rose)
Hardy, shorter varieties are most
suitable for containers. Grow in
sunny or semi-shaded position in
well-drained, medium-rich potting
mix. Water well during growing
season and feed weekly.

Scindapsus pictus
(Silver Vine)
Frost-tender, evergreen shrub with
climbing or trailing habit. Plant
outdoors in summer pots, tubs,
and terracotta wall baskets. Grows
particularly well in sheltered,
semi-shady sites in well-drained,
medium-rich potting mix.

Senecio maritima
(Senecio)
Frost-tender, evergreen sub-shrub grown for its feathery silver leaves. Enjoys sunny position in well-drained, medium-rich potting mix. *(See also Succulents.)*

Skimmia
Evergreen shrubs carrying attractive clusters of flower-buds in autumn, often in conjunction with berries. Sweet-scented flowers open in spring. Grow in semi-shade in well-drained, rich potting mix. Water well.

Solanum pseudocapsicum
(Winter Cherry)
Evergreen shrub grown as winter annual for its berries. Cultivars produce red, orange, white, and yellow berries. Grow in sheltered location in sun in well-drained, medium-rich potting mix.

Syringa meyeri
(Miniature Lilac)
Low-growing, deciduous shrub with small, sweet-scented lilac-pink flowers in late spring and early summer. Grow in sun in alkaline-rich potting mix.

Thymus
(Thyme)
Evergreen, matt-forming and dome-shaped sub-shrubs. Plant in sunny location in well-drained, medium-rich potting mix.

Viburnum tinus
(Viburnum)
Evergreen shrub with clusters of white flushed-pink flowers during winter and spring. Grow in well-drained, medium-rich potting mix in sun or semi-shade.

BAMBOO AND FERNS

Adiantum
(Maidenhair Fern)
Frost-tender ferns with delicate feathery green fronds. Plant in rich potting mix and site in sheltered position in semi-shade.

Pogonathemum paniceum
(Bamboo Grass)
Frost-tender, miniature bamboo grass with distinctive pink leaf tips. Grow in bright semi-shade in medium-rich potting mix.

Polypodium vulgare
(Creeping Fern)
Evergreen creeping fern with lacy fronds. Grow in shade or semi-shade in well-drained, medium-rich potting mix. Most ferns thrive in damp environments.

Polystichum aculeatum
(Hard Shield Fern)
Evergreen or semi-evergreen fern with bright green fronds. Grow in semi-shade or shade in well-drained rich potting mix, and keep the planting moist.

PERENNIALS

Ajuga reptans
(Ajuga; Bugle)
Evergreen, spreading perennial with deep purple leaves and spikes of intense blue-violet flowers in spring. Plant in medium-rich potting mix and grow in either sunny or shady site.

Aster novi-belgii
(Michaelmas Daisy)
Autumn-flowering perennial with small daisy flowers in red, pink, violet, purple, and white. Grow in sun or bright shade in well-drained, medium-rich potting mix.

Begonia
Genus divided into several groups, including Semperflorens (half-hardy annuals) and Tuberous (annuals). Tender, evergreens producing masses of flowers in all colours, except blue, throughout summer and autumn. Grow in shade or semi-shade in medium-rich potting mix. Feed weekly. Propagate by seed, stem cuttings, or division of tubers.

Campanula poscharskyana
(Campanula)
Evergreen, spreading hardy perennial with pale lilac flowers in summer. Grow in medium-rich soil in sun or semi-shade.

Chlorophytum comosum
(Spider Plant)
Frost-tender, evergreen perennial with fountain of thin variegated leaves. Useful for outdoor summer plantings and as houseplant. Grow in medium-rich potting mix in semi-shade or shade.

Chrysanthemum (Dendranthemum)
Genus of perennials and annuals with daisy-like flowers in many colours. 'Charm' chrysanthemums flower in autumn and are good for pot culture. Grow in medium-rich potting mix in sun or semi-shade.

Convolvulus sabatius
(Convolvulus)
Perennial with trailing habit. Host of purple-blue trumpet-shaped flowers in summer and autumn months. Grow in sunny location in sheltered site in well-drained, medium-rich potting mix.

Cymbalaria muralis
(Ivy-leaved Toadflax)
Creeping hardy perennial with ivy-shaped leaves and tiny purple flowers. Good in containers as underplanting for taller shrubs. Grow in any potting mix.

Erigeron
Perennials producing masses of pink, purple, and lilac daisy-like flowers throughout summer. Grow in sun in medium-rich potting mix. Feed fortnightly.

Gaillardia x grandiflora
(Blanket Flower)
Perennial with long succession of orange and yellow daisy flowers in summer. Grow in well-drained, medium-rich potting mix in sunny position. Keep well-watered and feed once a week.

Gentiana sino-ornata
(Gentian)
Frost-hardy, spreading, evergreen perennial with true blue flowers in autumn. Grow in sheltered position, in sun or semi-shade, in acid potting mix. Keep well-watered in growing season.

Heuchera
Frost-hardy, evergreen perennial with rosettes of leaves in green, purple, and silver. Grow in shade or semi-shade in medium-rich potting mix. Water well.

Houttuynia cordata
(Houttuynia)
Vigorous perennial with pink-, cream-, and gold-variegated leaves. Grow in semi-shady sites and keep well watered.

Iresine lindenii
(Blood Leaf)
Frost-tender perennial grown for its colourful leaves. Remove flower spikes as they appear, to encourage healthy foliage. Grow in medium-rich potting mix, in bright light to retain leaf colour.

Lysimachia nummularia
(Lysimachia)
Golden-leaved, trailing perennial with buttercup-like flowers in summer. Grow in sun or semi-shade in medium-rich potting mix in hanging baskets.

Mirabilis jalapa
(Marvel of Peru)
Tuberous perennial with scented flowers, in red, pink, white, and yellow, from mid-summer until autumn. Remove tubers from soil in autumn and store indoors over winter months.

Origanum onites
(Pot Marjoram)
Aromatic herb grown in pots or as a houseplant. Grow in sun in well-drained, medium-rich potting mix.

Origanum vulgare
(Oregano)
Frost-hardy, aromatic herb whose delicate, spicy flavour is used for cooking. Grow in sunny site in well-drained, medium-rich alkaline potting mix. Cut back old plant stems during spring.

Osteospermum
Short-lived evergreen perennials usually grown as annuals. Species have flowers in pink, purple, white, and yellow, some with quilled petals. Grow in sun in well-drained, medium-rich potting mix for flowers in summer and autumn months.

Oxalis lobata
(Oxalis)
Fast-growing perennial with clover-like leaves and yellow flowers in summer and autumn. Grow in well-drained medium-rich potting mix in sunny position and shelter in cold weather. Good for summer hanging baskets.

Paphiopedilum callosum
(Slipper Orchid)
Frost-tender, evergreen orchid with veined white flowers borne on tall, thin stems in spring and summer. Grow indoors in cool conservatory or garden room. Plant in bark chippings or orchid potting mix in semi-shade. Feed fortnightly.

Phalaenopsis equestris
(Epiphytic Orchid)
Frost-tender perennials with flamboyant flowers; best grown in orchid potting mix in bright shade in conservatory or garden room.

Plectranthus coleoides
(Plectranthus)
Frost-tender, trailing, evergreen perennial often grown as annual, with wavy-edged variegated leaves. Grow in medium-rich potting mix in any site. Cut back straggly growth as necessary to keep foliage healthy and bushy.

Polygonum
Several species suitable for growing in containers available, particularly the frost-tender *P.* 'Victory Carpet' with long-lasting clusters of pink flowers. Grow in medium-rich potting mix in any site. Keep well watered during growing season.

Primula

Hardy to frost-tender. Many species, particularly *P. vulgaris* (primrose), *P. veris* (cowslip), and their offspring, *P. denticulata* and *P. obconica*, make good container plants. Grow in semi-shady site in well-drained, rich potting mix. Keep well watered.

Ranunculus asiaticus
(Persian Buttercup)

Summer-flowering perennials with flowers similar to small peonies in red, pink, yellow, and white, early in season. Grow in sheltered position in sunny or semi-shaded position in well-drained, rich potting mix. Keep well watered.

Sagina glabra
(Pearlwort)

Matt-forming perennial that looks similar to moss, with tiny stems of white flowers in summer. Grow in sun or semi-shade in medium-rich potting mix. Use as underplanting for shrubs in containers.

Salvia
Sage

The frost-hardy herb, *S. officinalis* and the half-hardy perennial, *S. splendens*, and its cultivars make good pot plants. Grow in sun in well-drained, medium-rich potting mix. Feed fortnightly during growing season.

Saxifraga
(Saxifrage)

Rosette-forming perennials. Mossy varieties have pale flowers on tall, thin stems in late spring, and grow in any well-drained soil in shade or semi-shade.

Scabiosa caucasica
(Scabious)

Perennial producing masses of pink flowers from early summer until autumn. Grow in sun or semi-shade in medium-rich potting mix. Deadhead regularly or, for attractive seedheads, allow flowers to go to seed.

Scaevola emula
(Scaevola)

Frost-tender, summer-flowering annual producing flowering spikes of lavender-blue flowers over long period. Grow in medium-rich potting mix in sunny position.

Tolmiea menziesii
(Pick-a-back Plant)

Evergreen perennial grown as houseplant. Baby plants grow on top of leaves. Plant in medium-rich potting mix in shady site. Water well in summer months.

Tradescantia fluminensis
(Tradescantia; Wandering Jew)

Frost-tender, evergreen perennial grown for its ornamental foliage. Plant in shady or semi-shaded site in well-drained, medium-rich potting mix.

Vinca major
(Greater Periwinkle)

Hardy, evergreen perennials with trailing habit and blue or white flowers in spring and summer months. Grow in semi-shaded site in medium-rich potting mix.

Viola
(Pansy and Violet)

Low-growing perennial used as an annual. Grow in semi-shade or sun in well-drained, rich potting mix. Water and fertilize with high potash content plant food during growing season.

Zantedeschia
(Arum Lily)

Frost-tender, tuberous perennials *Z. aethiopica* has white spathes and *Z. rehmannii* has pink spathes in spring and summer. Grow in well-drained, rich potting mix, in semi-shade, in sheltered position.

Zebrina pendula
(Zebrina)

Similar to *Tradescantia fluminensis*, this tender, trailing perennial has purple and silver leaves. Grow in semi-shade in well-drained, medium-rich potting mix.

ANNUALS

Ageratum houstonianum
(Floss Flower)

Annual with lilac-blue, pink, or white flowers. Plant in sun in well-drained, medium-rich potting mix. Feed weekly in summer and dead-head regularly.

Antirrhinum majus
(Snapdragon)

Perennial best grown as annual. Varieties available in red, pink, orange, yellow, and white. Plant in sun in well-drained, medium-rich potting mix. Feed weekly in flowering season. Water well.

Bellis perennis
(Double Daisy)

Biennial usually grown as annual. Produces large numbers of double daisy flowers in spring and early summer in white, red, and pink. Plant in well-drained, medium-rich potting mix, and grow in sun or semi-shade. Deadhead blooms regularly to increase amount of flowers produced.

Brachycome iberidifolia
(Swan River Daisy)

Hardy, bushy annual with green leaves and blue, lilac, or pink daisy-like flowers in summer and early autumn. Plant in sun or semi-shade in medium-rich potting mix. Feed weekly.

Coleus blumei
(Coleus)

Frost-tender, bushy, evergreen perennial grown as annual for its ornamental, brightly coloured leaves. Plant in well-drained, medium-rich potting mix in bright shade. Feed fortnightly. Remove flower spikes as they appear for best leaf colour.

Cosmos 'Sunny Gold'

Bushy annual with feathery leaves and large golden flowerheads in summer and early autumn. Plant in sun in well-drained, medium-rich potting mix.

Delphinium consolida
(Larkspur)

Summer-flowering annual with spires of flowers in true blue, pink, and white. Plant in sun in well-drained, medium-rich potting mix. Feed once a week.

Diascia

Slightly tender perennials grown as annuals, producing succession of pink flowers throughout summer and autumn. Grow in well-drained, medium-rich potting mix in sun or semi-shade. Good for hanging baskets.

Eustoma grandiflorum
(Prairie Gentian)

Annual with silver-green leaves, producing succession of pink, lilac, and pure white blooms during summer months. Grow in well-drained, rich potting mix in sunny site, and feed weekly.

Impatiens
(Busy Lizzie)

Frost-tender annuals producing wealth of red, pink, orange, and white single and double blooms from early summer until first frosts. Grow in sun, semi-shade, or shade in well-drained medium-rich potting mix and keep well watered. Feed weekly.

Lobelia erinus
(Lobelia)

Summer-flowering annual, either trailing or low mounding. True blue, as well as pink, lilac, and white, varieties available; good for filling out window boxes, hanging baskets, sinks, and troughs.

Lotus berthelotii
(Lotus)

Frost-tender, trailing perennial usually grown as annual. Produces scarlet flowers in good summers, but worth growing just for its silver-green foliage. Plant in medium-rich potting mix in sun. Water well in growing season.

Monopsis lutea
(Lutea)

Frost-tender, evergreen trailing perennial grown as annual with small green leaves and yellow gorse-like flowers. Plant in sun in well-drained, medium-rich potting mix and feed weekly.

Ocimum basilicum
(Basil)

Frost-tender perennial grown as annual. Grow in sun in medium-rich potting mix. Several varieties available with good flavour and attractive leaf colour.

Pelargonium

Frost-tender, evergreen perennials mostly grown as annuals. Excellent as pot plants. Flowers in reds, purples, pinks, oranges, and white. Available as trailing (ivy-leaved) and upright (zonal) varieties and those with sweet-scented foliage. Grow in sun or semi-shade in medium-rich potting mix. Water well in flowering season. Feed weekly.

Petroselinum crispum
(Parsley)

Biennial best grown as annual. Plant in sun or semi-shade in well-drained, rich potting mix.

Petunia x hybrida
(Petunia)

Perennials grown as summer-flowering annuals with large trumpet-shaped flowers in white, yellow, red, pink, lilac, and purple. Grow in medium-rich potting mix in sun. Feed weekly.

Phacelia campanularia
(Phacelia)

Moderately fast-growing, hardy, bushy annual with intense true blue, bell-shaped flowers in summer and autumn. Grow in sun in rich potting mix.

Phlox

Low-growing species, such as *P. drummondii*, have pink, white, red, blue, purple, and lilac flowers in summer, and are well suited to pot culture. Plant in well-drained, medium-rich potting mix in sun or semi-shade. Feed once a week with high potash content food.

Reinwardtia trigyna
(Reinwardtia)
Frost-tender, low-growing annual with white flowers in summer. Grow in sun or semi-shade in medium-rich potting mix. Water well during growing season; good for hanging basket displays.

Tagetes
(Marigold)
Annuals such as *T. erecta* and *T. patula* with orange flowers in summer and autumn. Grow in sun in medium-rich potting mix.

Tropaeolum majus
(Nasturtium)
Fast-growing, bushy annual with red, orange, or yellow flowers for several months. Grow in sun in well-drained potting mix. Dead-head regularly for best results.

Verbena x *hybrida*
(Verbena)
Summer-flowering perennial grown as annual with clusters of flowers in red, pink, apricot, and white. Grow in sun in medium-rich potting mix. Water well in summer and feed weekly.

BULBS, CORMS, AND TUBERS

Allium schoenoprasum
(Chives)
Clump-forming, summer-flowering bulb with narrow, erect, dark green leaves used for cooking. Grow in sunny location in well-drained, medium-rich potting mix.

Clivia miniata
(Clivia)
Frost-tender, rhizomatous perennial with decorative, strap-like leaves and heads of trumpet-shaped orange flowers. Grow in semi-shade in well-drained, medium-rich potting mix. Leave plant in container for several years where it will thrive as it enjoys being pot-bound.

Crocus vernus
(Crocus)
Frost-hardy, spring-flowering species for growing in containers. Choose from range of coloured varieties. Plant in medium-rich potting mix in sun or semi-shade.

Cyclamen
Hardy to frost-tender tubers producing flowers, in autumn, winter, or spring, in red, pink, and white. *C. coum*, *C. cyprium* and *C. hederifolium* are hardy. *C. persicum* produces tender florists' varieties.

Dahlia
Frost-tender, tuberous perennials producing single and double flowers in vibrant and pastel colours. Plant in sun in medium-rich potting mix. Water freely and feed once a week.

Fritillaria meleagris
(Snake's-head Fritillary)
Spring-flowering bulbs with bell-shaped flowers distinguished by snakeskin markings. Plant in sun or semi-shade in well-drained, medium-rich potting mix, and plant out into grass after flowering to naturalize in the garden.

Hyacinthus
(Hyacinth)
Frost-hardy, spring-flowering bulbs, mostly scented; ideal for pot culture both indoors and outdoors. Grow in sun or semi-shade in well-drained, medium-rich potting mix.

Iris reticulata
(Reticulata Iris)
Spring-flowering miniature iris with sweet scent. Plant bulbs in sun or semi-shade. Grow in well-drained, medium-rich potting mix and keep just moist during winter.

Lilium
(Lily)
Mainly summer-flowering bulbs, many with scented, trumpet-shaped blooms in variety of colours. Grow in sun or semi-shade in rich potting mix. Water well and feed once a week with a high potash content plant food.

Muscari
(Grape Hyacinth)
Spring-flowering bulbs with scented blue spires of flowers. Grow in well-drained, medium-rich potting mix in sunny site. Keep just moist through winter, but withhold water if temperature drops below freezing.

Narcissus
Spring-flowering bulbs. Popular cultivars, such as 'Paper White' and 'Soleil d'Or' are ideal for indoor displays. For outdoor displays choose sweetly scented narcissus, such as *N.* 'Trevithian', *N.* 'Silver Chimes', *N. jonquilla*, and *N. poeticus*. Plant in sun or semi-shady site in well-drained, medium-rich potting mix.

Scilla
Spring-flowering bulbs with blue or white flowers. Plant the bulbs in autumn and grow in sun or semi-shade in well-drained, medium-rich potting mix.

Tulipa
(Tulip)
Spring-flowering bulbs in many colours. Grow in sun or semi-shade in medium-rich potting mix. Plant in autumn. Keep soil just moist throughout winter, but withhold water if temperature falls below freezing.

CACTI AND OTHER SUCCULENTS

Crassula lycopodioides
(Crassula)
Frost-tender, pale grey-stemmed succulent with insignificant leaves. Grow indoors in bright site, in well-drained, medium-rich potting mix with equal quantity of coarse sand added. Water sparingly.

Echeveria harmsii
(Echeveria)
Frost-tender, silver-leaved succulent usually grown as houseplant. Thrives outdoors in summer, if located in sunny sheltered site. Plant in gritty potting mix and water sparingly.

Gasteria verrucosa
(Gasteria)
Frost-tender succulent with fleshy, green, white-spotted leaves. Grow in bright site in well-drained, medium-rich potting mix with grit added. Keep planting fairly dry during winter.

Haworthia attenuata
(Haworthia)
Frost-tender, fleshy succulent with triangular, smooth green leaves with attractive silver markings. Grow in bright shade in well-drained, medium-rich potting mix.

Kalanchoe
Frost-tender, evergreen succulents with fleshy leaves and showy red, pink, and yellow flowerheads in spring. *K. pumila* has silver velvety leaves and pink flowers in spring. Excellent as indoor plants.

Nopalxochia phyllanthoides
(Epiphytic Cactus)
Frost-tender, perennial cactus with flattish stems producing lily-shaped pink flowers in spring. Grow indoors in warm, light situation in rich potting mix. Feed fortnightly in late summer and autumn. Keep just moist in winter.

Sedum
(Stonecrop)
Evergreen succulents with pink and yellow flowers, mostly in summer and autumn. Many, such as *S. acre* and *S. spathulifolium*, grow well in alpine troughs. Plant in sun in medium-rich potting mix.

Sempervivum
(Houseleek)
Rosette-forming, evergreen perennials grown for their fleshy leaves in alpine troughs and low pans. Grow outdoors in sun, in sheltered position and plant in well-drained, gritty, low-nutrient potting mix.

Senecio
A large genus of plants including frost-tender succulents, *S. articulatus* and *S. kleinii*, with grey-blue stems and smooth, glossy leaves. Grow indoors in well-drained, medium-rich potting mix with added grit to aid drainage.
 S. greyii, a hardy, evergreen shrub, is grown in outdoor displays for its attractive silver leaves. Plant in sunny site in well-drained, medium-rich potting mix. (*See also Trees and Shrubs.*)

INDEX

ACKNOWLEDGMENTS

Author's Acknowledgments
Foremost thanks to my business partner Quentin Roake who, with his perceptive thoughts and great enthusiasm and energy, has shared in the creation of this book.

To photographer Matthew Ward for his splendid studio and location pictures and for always making all the work seem so easy.

To Bella Pringle and Louise Bruce, project editor and art editor, who, with their expertise and commitment, made this book on container gardening such fun to produce.

To Nick Lawrence of Landscape Management Construction for providing us with growing space and for watering the plantings.

To William Broadbent, Clifton Nurseries Ltd., May Cristea, Mrs Franklin and Sarah Franklin, Fiona Hervey, Pauline and Richard Lay, Jenny and Richard Raworth, and Mrs Reiss-Edwards, for allowing us to photograph our container plantings in their gardens.

Photographer's Acknowledgments
Steven Wooster, our additional location photographer, would also like to thank the following garden owners and designers for allowing their gardens and conservatories to be photographed for this book:
Beth Chatto, Mr and Mrs N. Coote,

Mrs Forrest, Mr and Mrs A. Huntington, Mr and Mrs J. Hilton, Mrs Ingram/Maria Dallow (Flowers Galore), Mr and Mrs Hugh Johnson, Prue and Martin Lane-Fox, Major and Mrs Mordaunt-Hare, Mr and Mrs C. Newman, Anthony Noel, Mr and Mrs Paice, Anthony Paul, Jenny and Richard Raworth, and Martin Summers.

Publisher's Acknowledgments
Dorling Kindersley would also like to thank: Alan Hemsley for invaluable help with plant identification; Super Scenes for painting the background for each season opener; Vanessa Luff and Debbie Myatt for illustrations; Irene Lyford for editorial help; Lesley Riley for proof-reading; Michael Allaby for the index.

Picture Credits
All photographs in this book were taken by Matthew Ward, with the exception of the following, listed below:
Peter Anderson 146b; 148b; 151t; 152b; 153b. **Lynne Brotchie (Garden Picture Library)** 8; 14br; 45t. **Jonathan Buckley** 98t; 138. **Brian Carter (Garden Picture Library)** 20. **John Glover (Garden Picture Library)** 16b; 18l. **Stephen Hayward** 9; 17bl; 26; 46; 52-53; 61; 64; 67; 73; 75; 94; 100; 116; 120; 130; 144. **Roger Hyam (Garden Picture Library)** 44; 45. **Diana Miller** 39; 40; 42; 51; 122tr. **Clive Nichols** 12t (The Old Rectory, Sudborough, Northants); 16t (The National Asthma Campaign Garden, Chelsea Flower Show 1993); 17t (The Old School House, Castle Hedingham) 77br (The Old Rectory, Sudborough, Northants); 84b (Butterstream, County Meath, Ireland. Designer: Jim Reynolds); 91t (17, Fulham Park Gardens, London, Designer: Anthony Noel); 105br (The Old School House, Castle Hedingham). **Gary Rogers (Garden Picture Library)** 25; 105t. **David Russell (Garden Picture Library)** 45br. **Ron Sutherland (Garden Picture Library)** 70b. **Juliette Wade (Garden Picture Library)** 15b; 18r. **Steven Wooster** 12b; 13tl; 13tr; 22t; 22b; 24; 38; 58t; 65t; 65br; 70; 77t; 77bl; 98b; 104; 122tl; 139.